Her Bark & Her Bite

JAMES ALBON

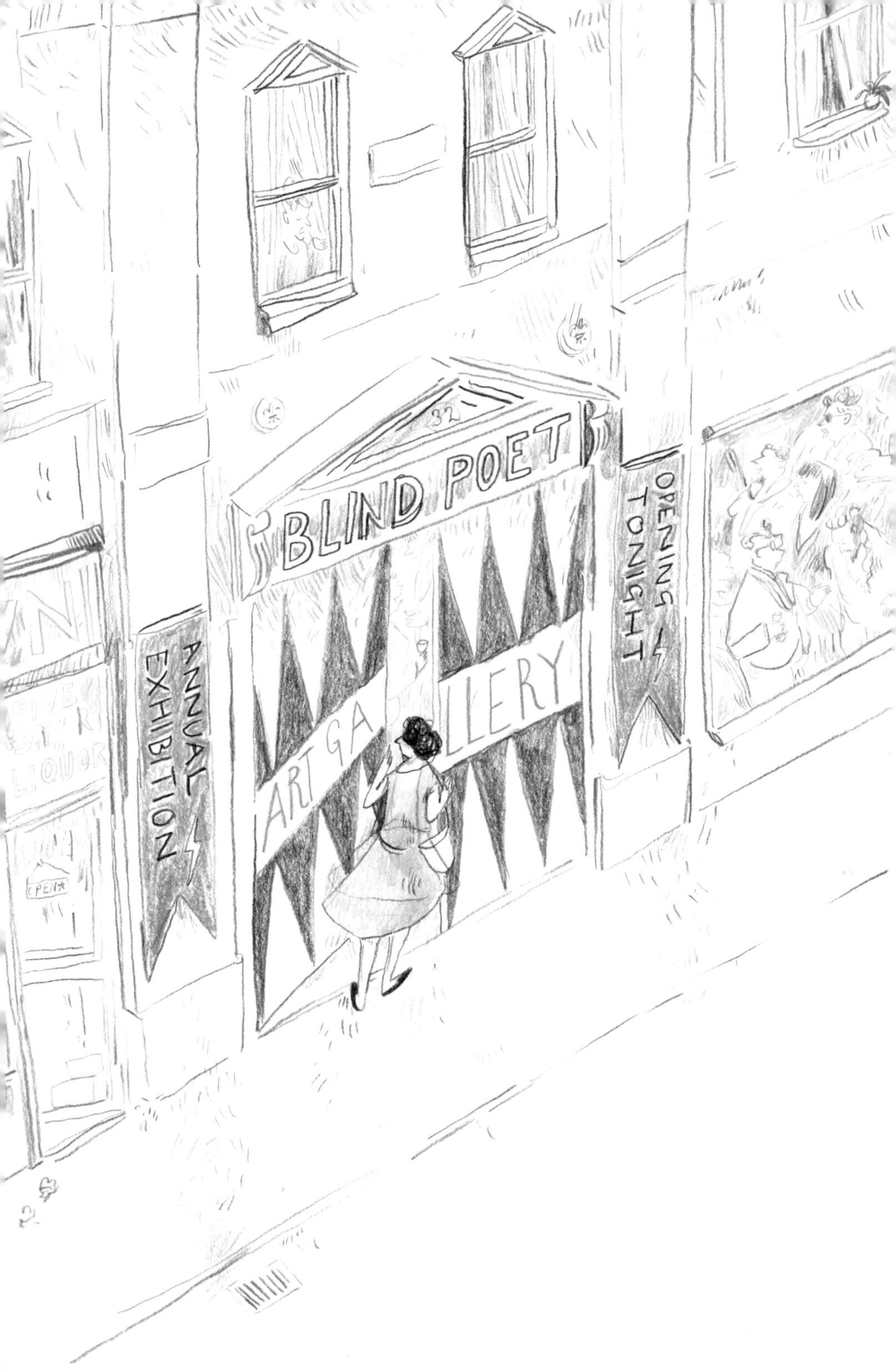
32
BLIND POET
ART GALLERY
ANNUAL EXHIBITION
OPENING TONIGHT
LIQUOR
OPEN

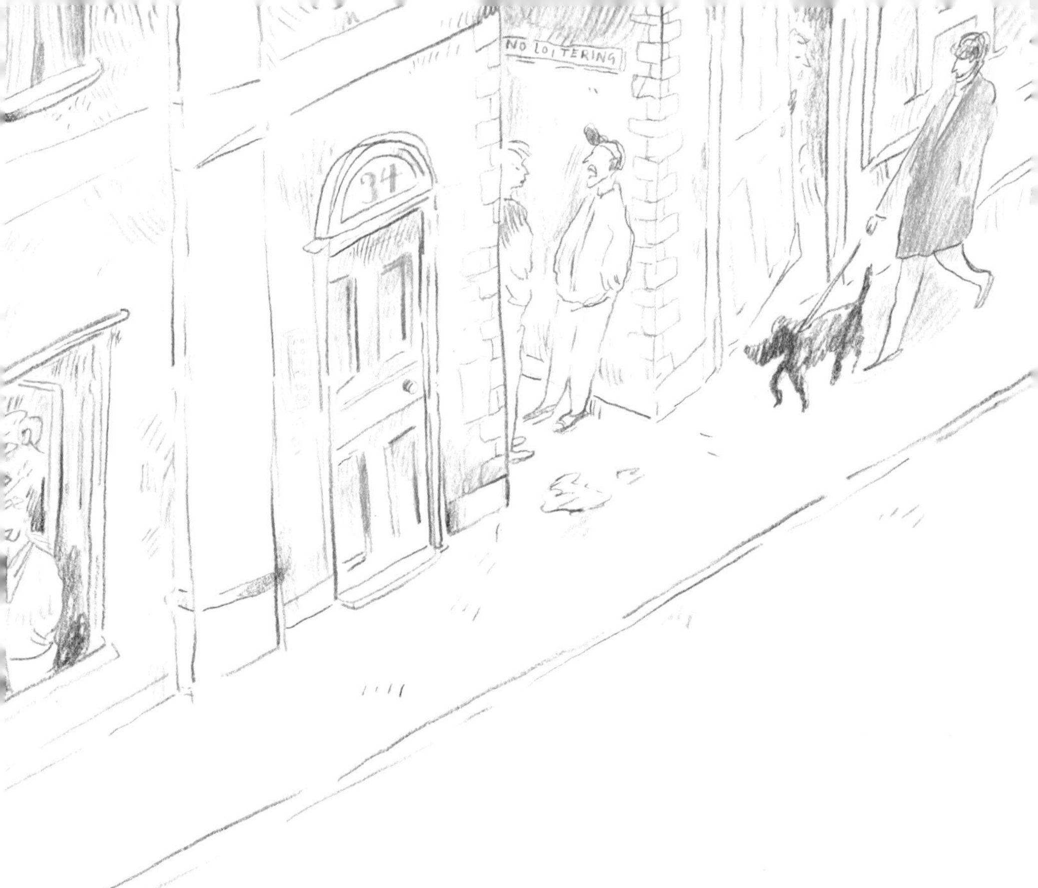
NO LOITERING
34

Her Bark & Her Bite

JAMES ALBON

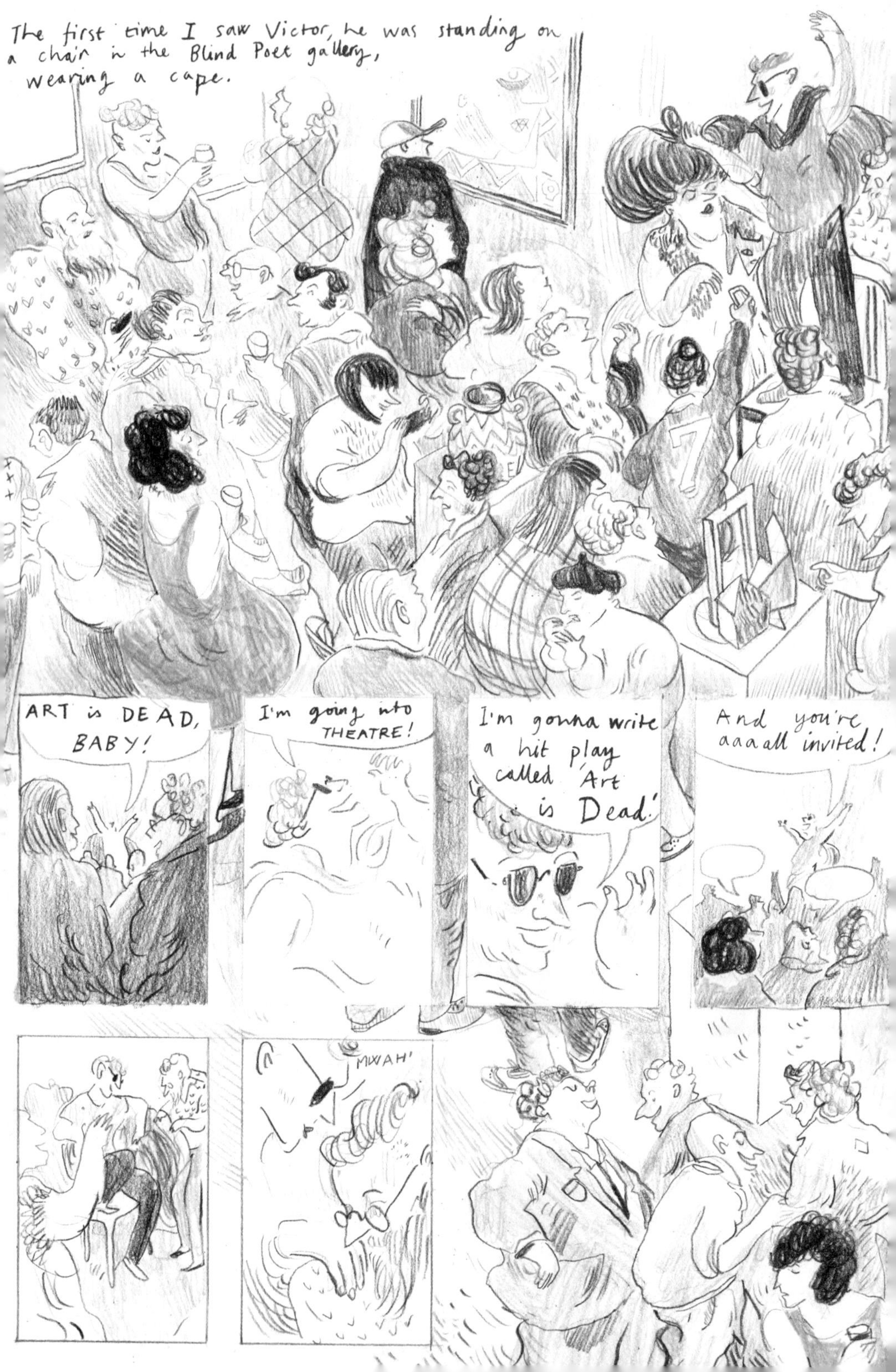
The first time I saw Victor, he was standing on a chair in the Blind Poet gallery, wearing a cape.
ART is DEAD, BABY!
I'm going into THEATRE!
I'm gonna write a hit play called 'Art is Dead.'
And you're aaaall invited!
MWAH!

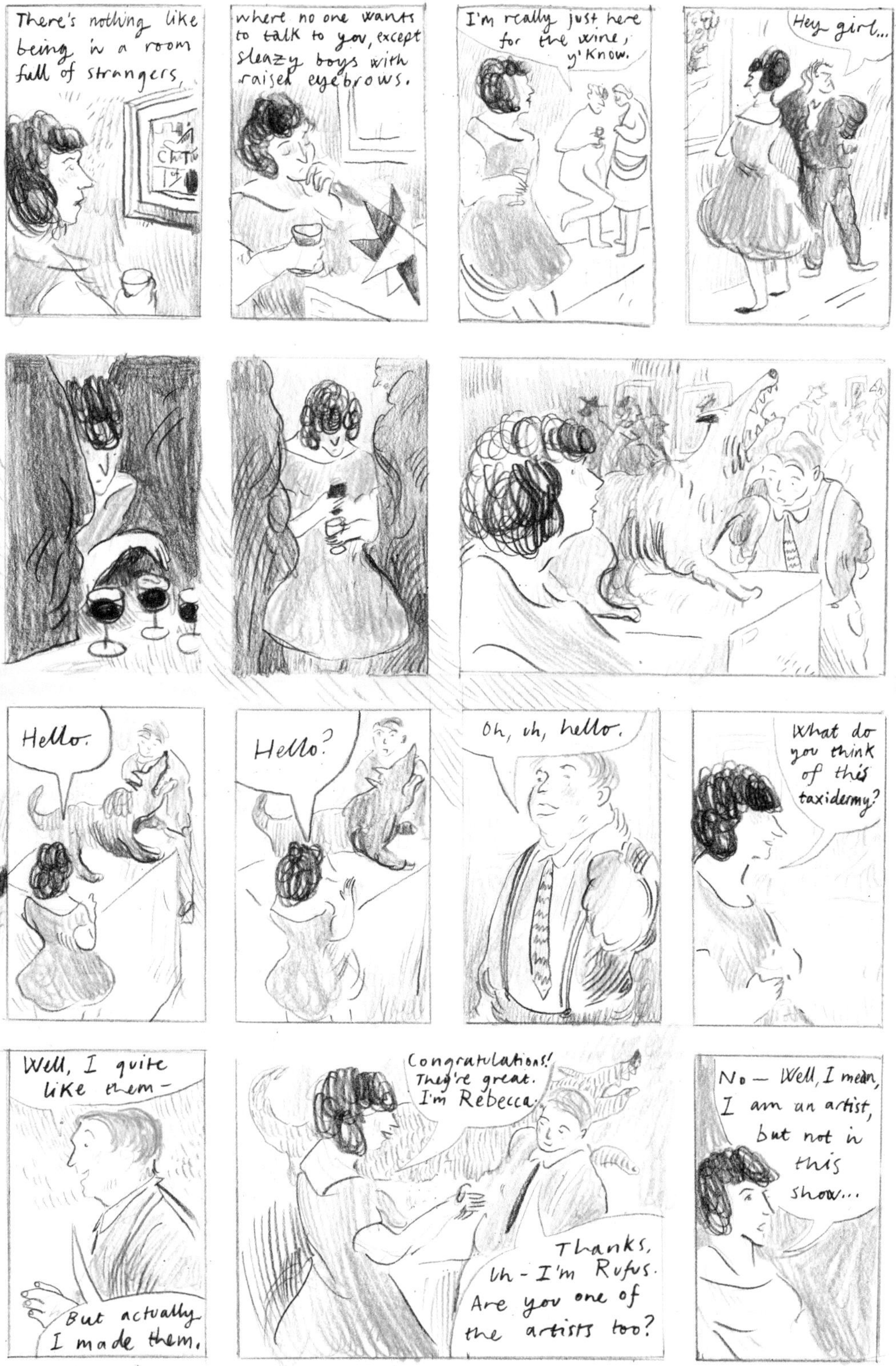
There's nothing like being in a room full of strangers,
where no one wants to talk to you, except sleazy boys with raised eyebrows.
I'm really just here for the wine, y'know.
Hey girl...
Hello.
Hello?
Oh, uh, hello.
What do you think of this taxidermy?
Well, I quite like them-
But actually I made them.
Congratulations! They're great. I'm Rebecca.
Thanks, uh- I'm Rufus. Are you one of the artists too?
No- Well, I mean, I am an artist, but not in this show...

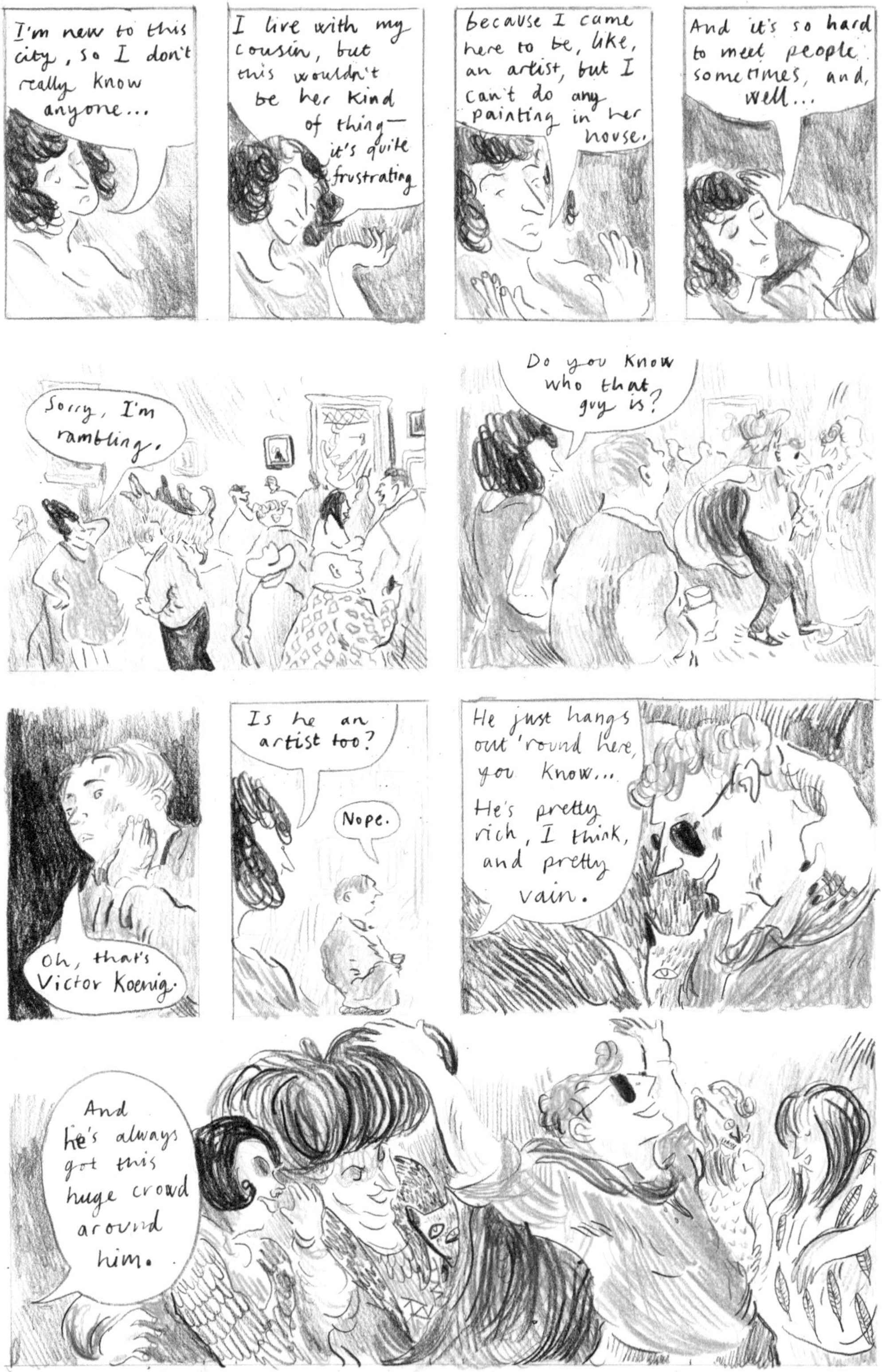
I'm new to this city, so I don't really know anyone...
I live with my cousin, but this wouldn't be her kind of thing— it's quite frustrating
because I came here to be, like, an artist, but I can't do any painting in her house.
And it's so hard to meet people sometimes, and, well...
Sorry, I'm rambling.
Do you know who that guy is?
Oh, that's Victor Koenig.
Is he an artist too?
Nope.
He just hangs out 'round here, you know...
He's pretty rich, I think, and pretty vain.
And he's always got this huge crowd around him.

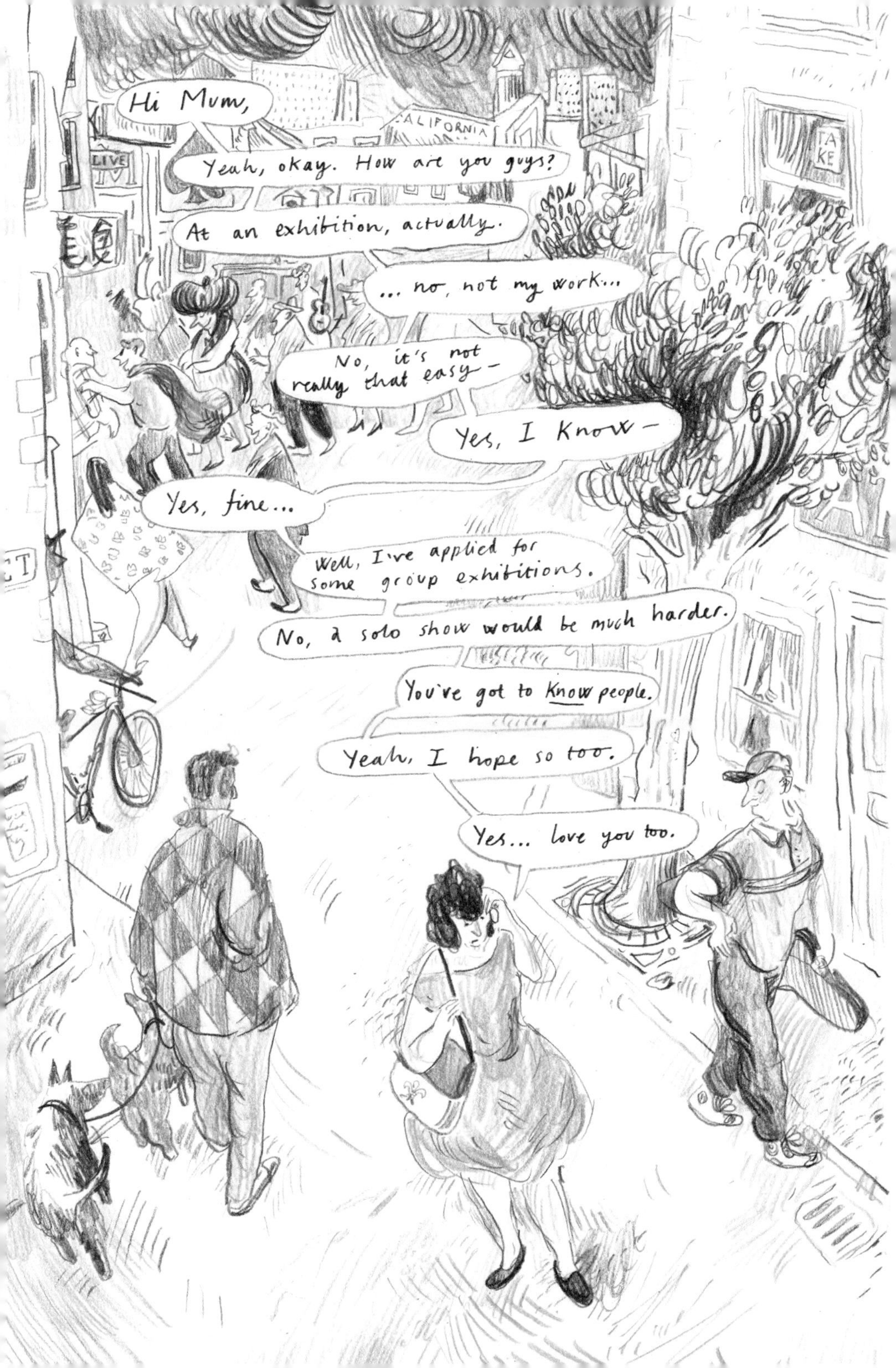
CALIFORNIA
LIVE
TAKE
Hi Mum,
Yeah, okay. How are you guys?
At an exhibition, actually.
... no, not my work...
No, it's not really that easy –
Yes, I know –
Yes, fine...
Well, I've applied for some group exhibitions.
No, a solo show would be much harder.
You've got to know people.
Yeah, I hope so too.
Yes... love you too.

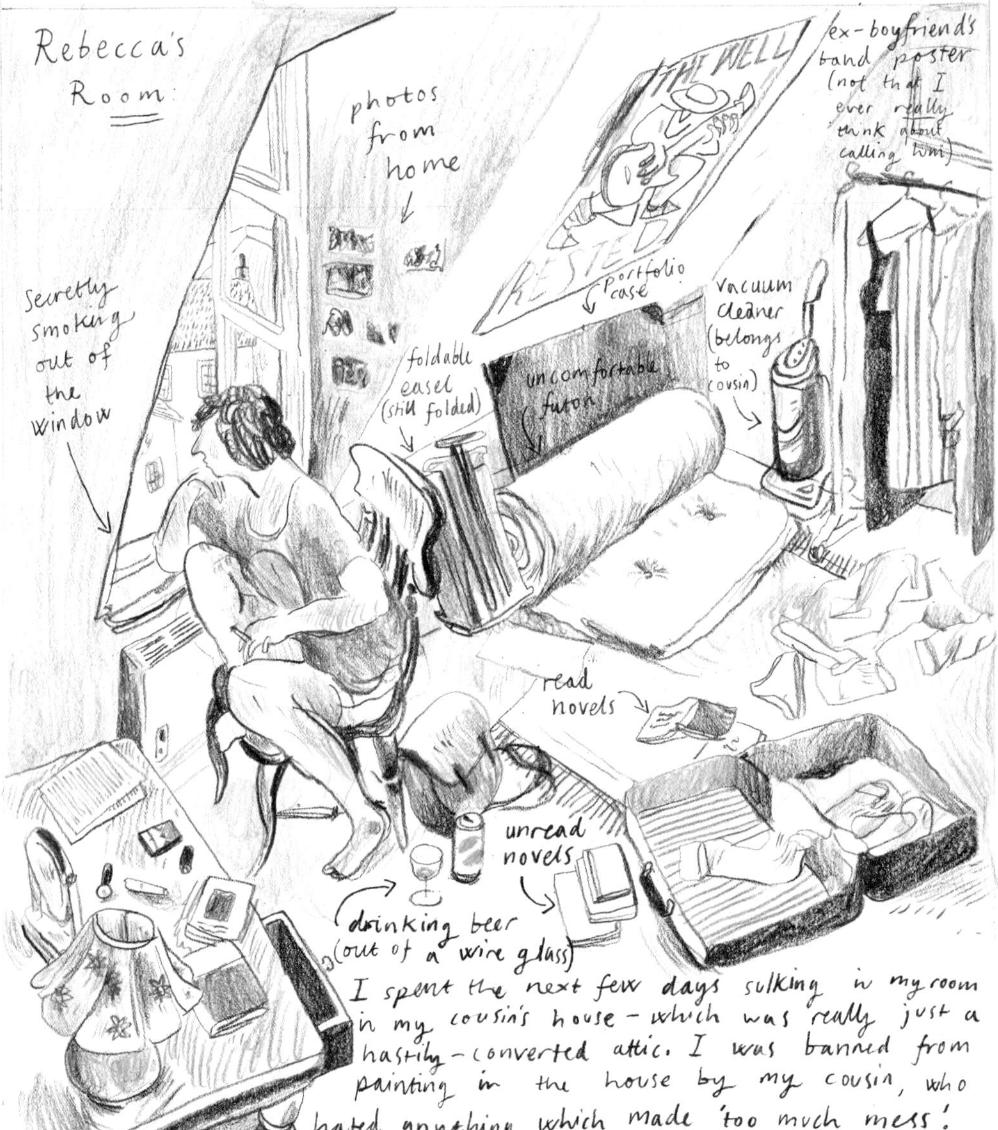
Rebecca's Room:
photos from home
THE WELL RESTED
ex-boyfriend's band poster (not that I ever really think about calling him)
secretly smoking out of the window
portfolio case
vacuum cleaner (belongs to cousin)
foldable easel (still folded)
uncomfortable futon
read novels
unread novels
drinking beer (out of a wine glass)
I spent the next few days sulking in my room in my cousin's house - which was really just a hastily-converted attic. I was banned from painting in the house by my cousin, who hated anything which made 'too much mess'.

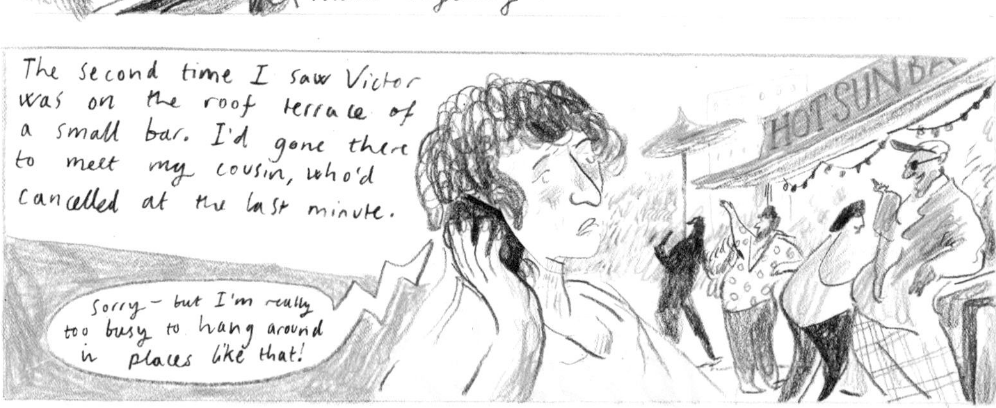
The second time I saw Victor was on the roof terrace of a small bar. I'd gone there to meet my cousin, who'd cancelled at the last minute.
HOT SUN
Sorry - but I'm really too busy to hang around in places like that!

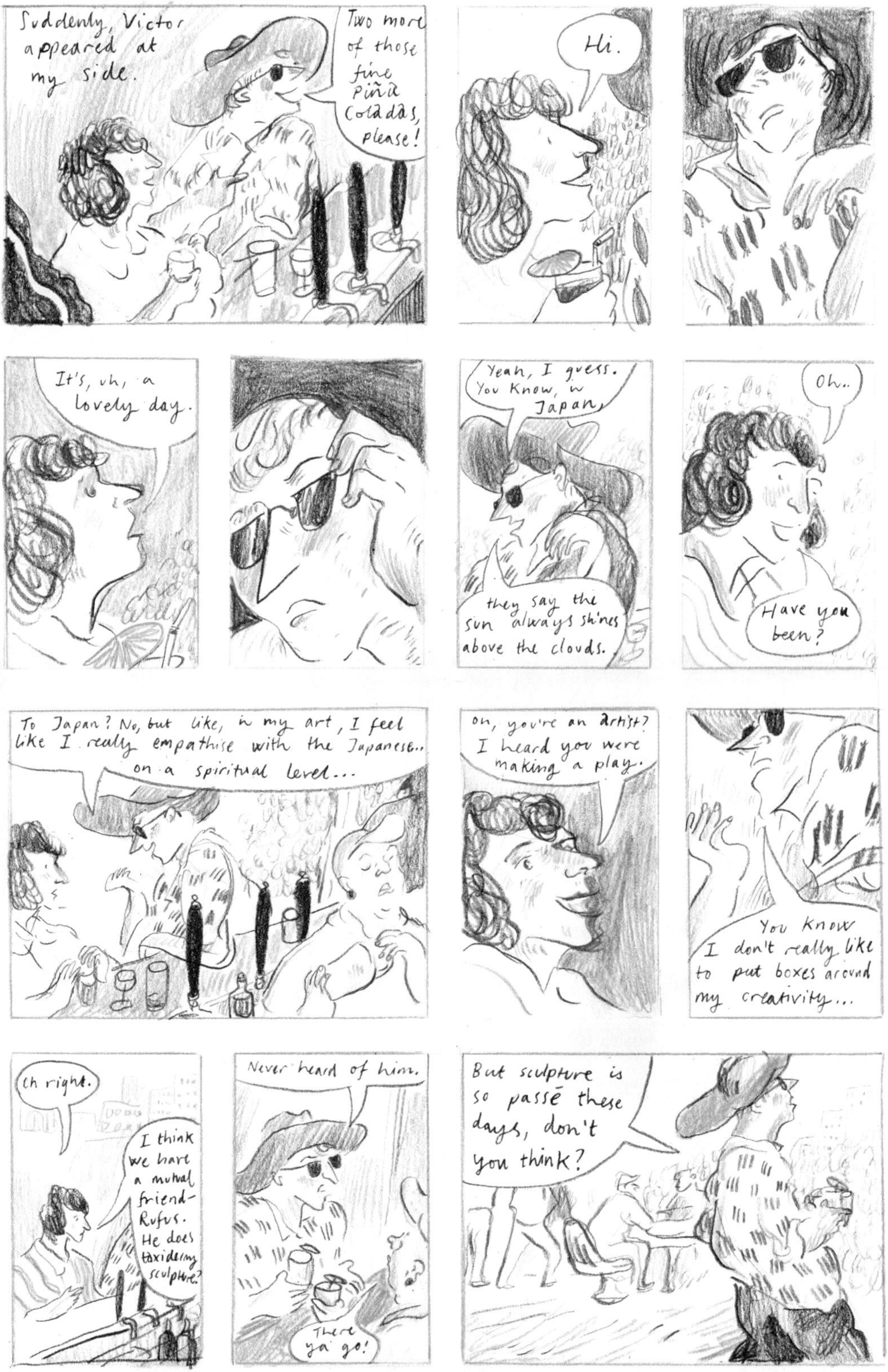
Suddenly, Victor appeared at my side.
Two more of those fine Piña Coladas, please!
Hi.
It's, uh, a lovely day.
Yeah, I guess. You know, in Japan,
they say the sun always shines above the clouds.
Oh..
Have you been?
To Japan? No, but like, in my art, I feel like I really empathise with the Japanese... on a spiritual level...
Oh, you're an artist? I heard you were making a play.
You know I don't really like to put boxes around my creativity...
Oh right.
I think we have a mutual friend- Rufus. He does taxidermy sculpture?
Never heard of him.
There ya' go!
But sculpture is so passé these days, don't you think?

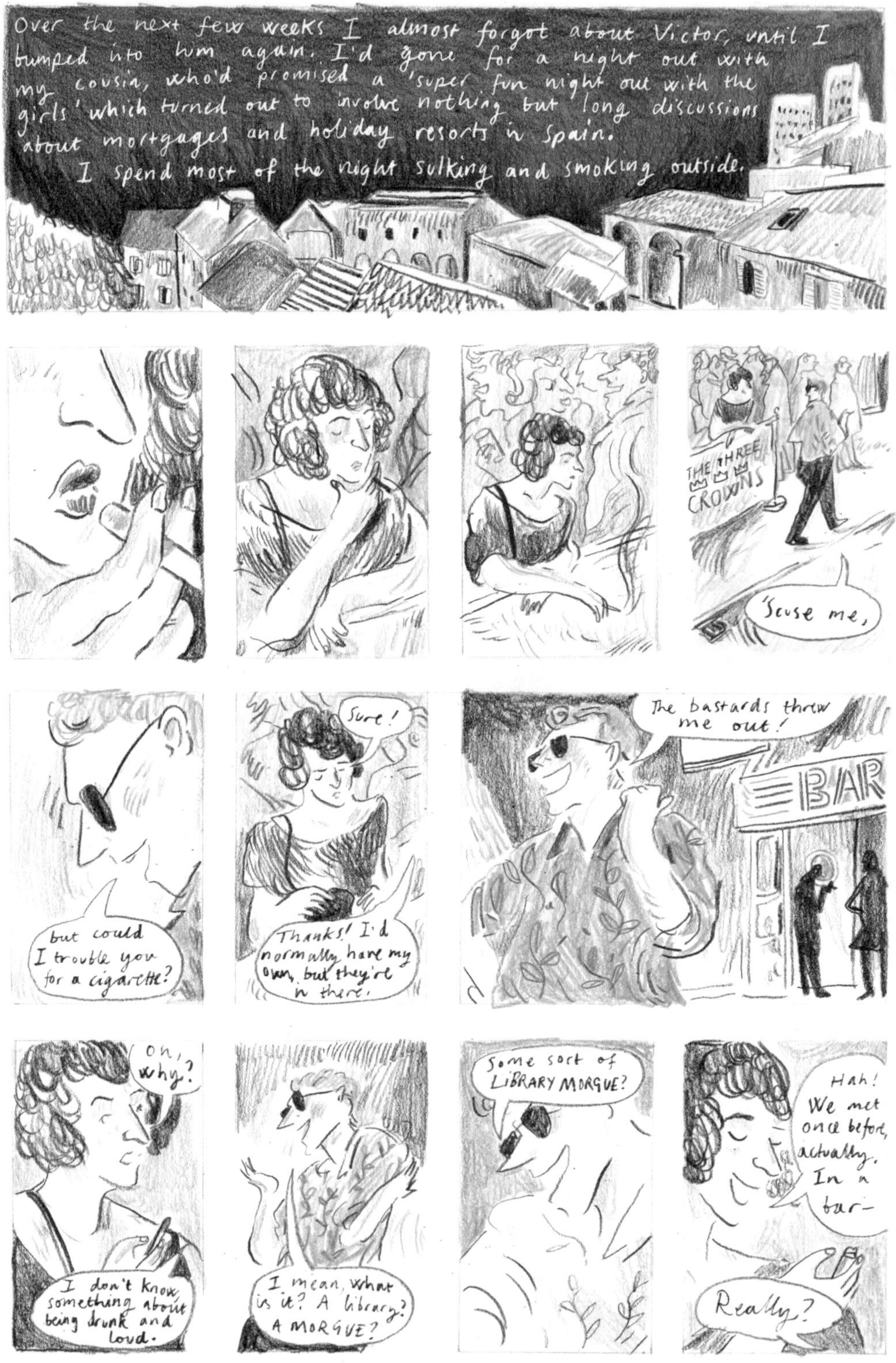
Over the next few weeks I almost forgot about Victor, until I bumped into him again. I'd gone for a night out with my cousin, who'd promised a 'super fun night out with the girls' which turned out to involve nothing but long discussions about mortgages and holiday resorts in Spain.
I spend most of the night sulking and smoking outside.
THE THREE CROWNS
'Scuse me,
but could I trouble you for a cigarette?
Sure!
Thanks! I'd normally have my own, but they're in there.
The bastards threw me out!
BAR
Oh, why?
I don't know, something about being drunk and loud.
I mean, what is it? A library? A MORGUE?
Some sort of LIBRARY MORGUE?
Hah! We met once before, actually. In a bar–
Really?

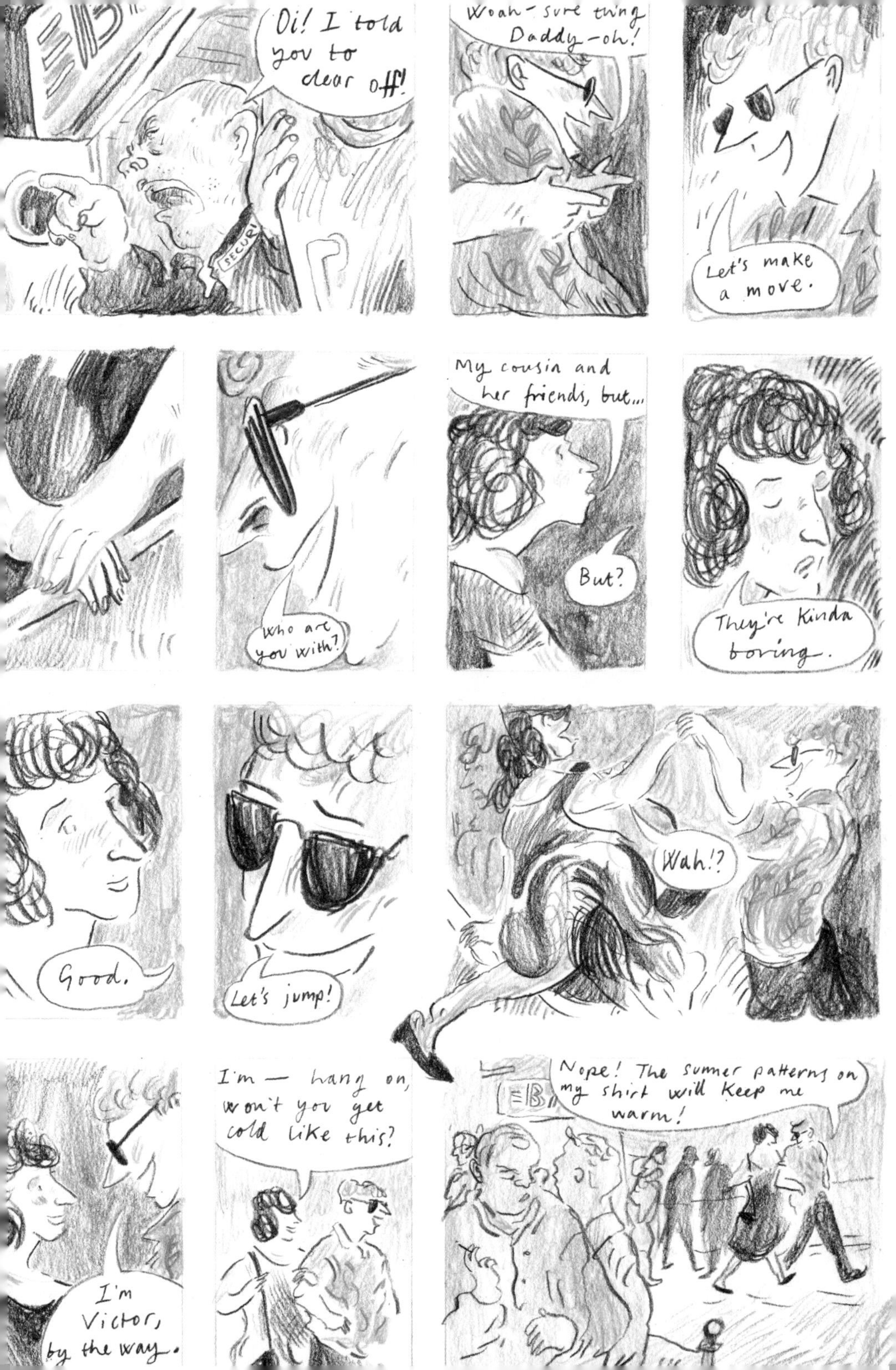
Oi! I told you to clear off!
Woah- sure thing Daddy-oh!
Let's make a move.
Who are you with?
My cousin and her friends, but...
But?
They're Kinda boring.
Good.
Let's jump!
Wah!?
I'm Victor, by the way.
I'm — hang on, won't you get cold like this?
Nope! The summer patterns on my shirt will Keep me warm!

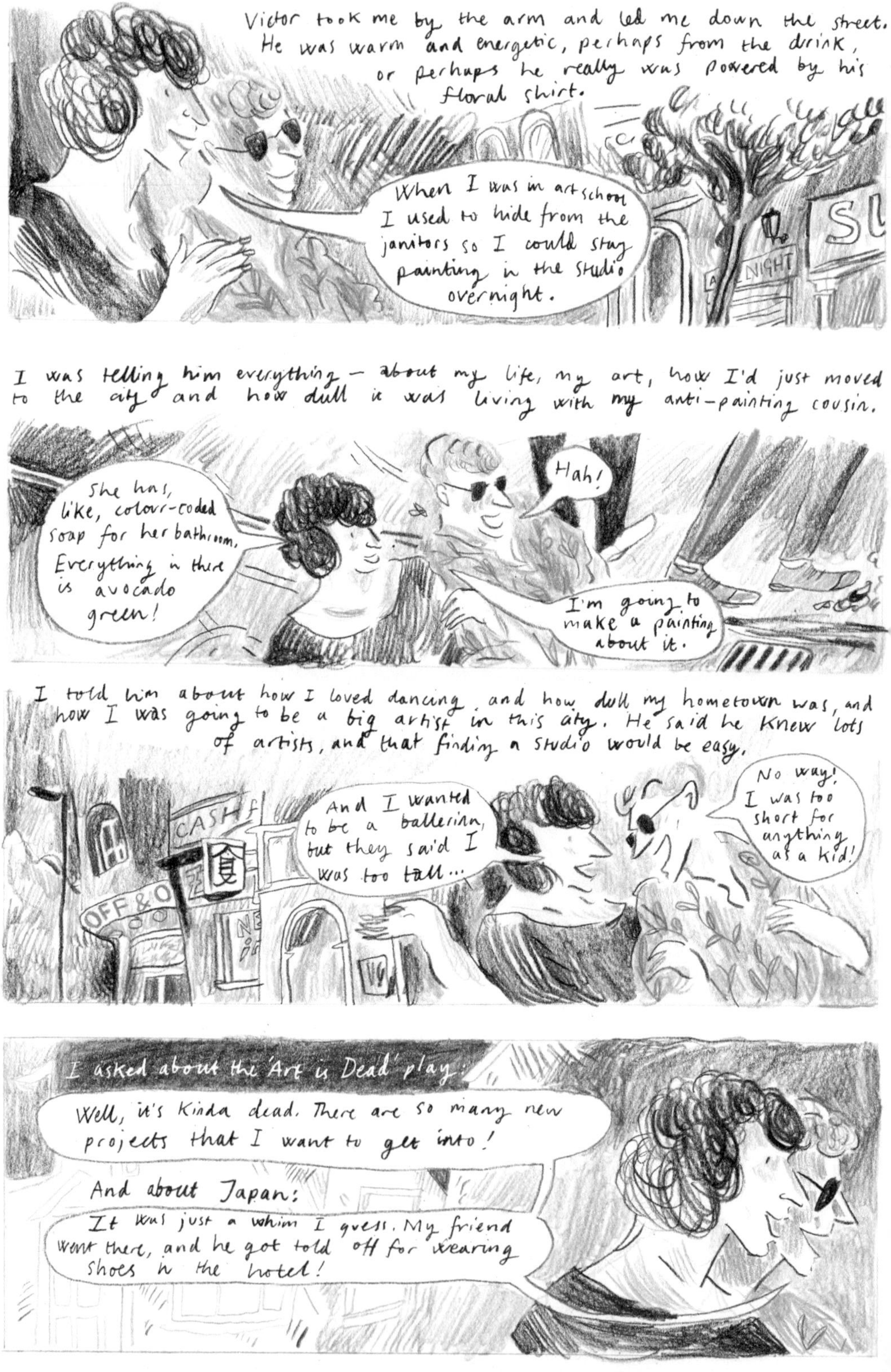
Victor took me by the arm and led me down the street. He was warm and energetic, perhaps from the drink, or perhaps he really was powered by his floral shirt.
When I was in art school I used to hide from the janitors so I could stay painting in the studio overnight.
SU
NIGHT
I was telling him everything – about my life, my art, how I'd just moved to the city and how dull it was living with my anti-painting cousin.
She has, like, colour-coded soap for her bathroom. Everything in there is avocado green!
Hah!
I'm going to make a painting about it.
I told him about how I loved dancing and how dull my hometown was, and how I was going to be a big artist in this city. He said he knew lots of artists, and that finding a studio would be easy.
And I wanted to be a ballerina, but they said I was too tall...
No way! I was too short for anything as a kid!
CASH
食
OFF & O
I asked about the 'Art is Dead' play:
Well, it's kinda dead. There are so many new projects that I want to get into!
And about Japan:
It was just a whim I guess. My friend went there, and he got told off for wearing shoes in the hotel!

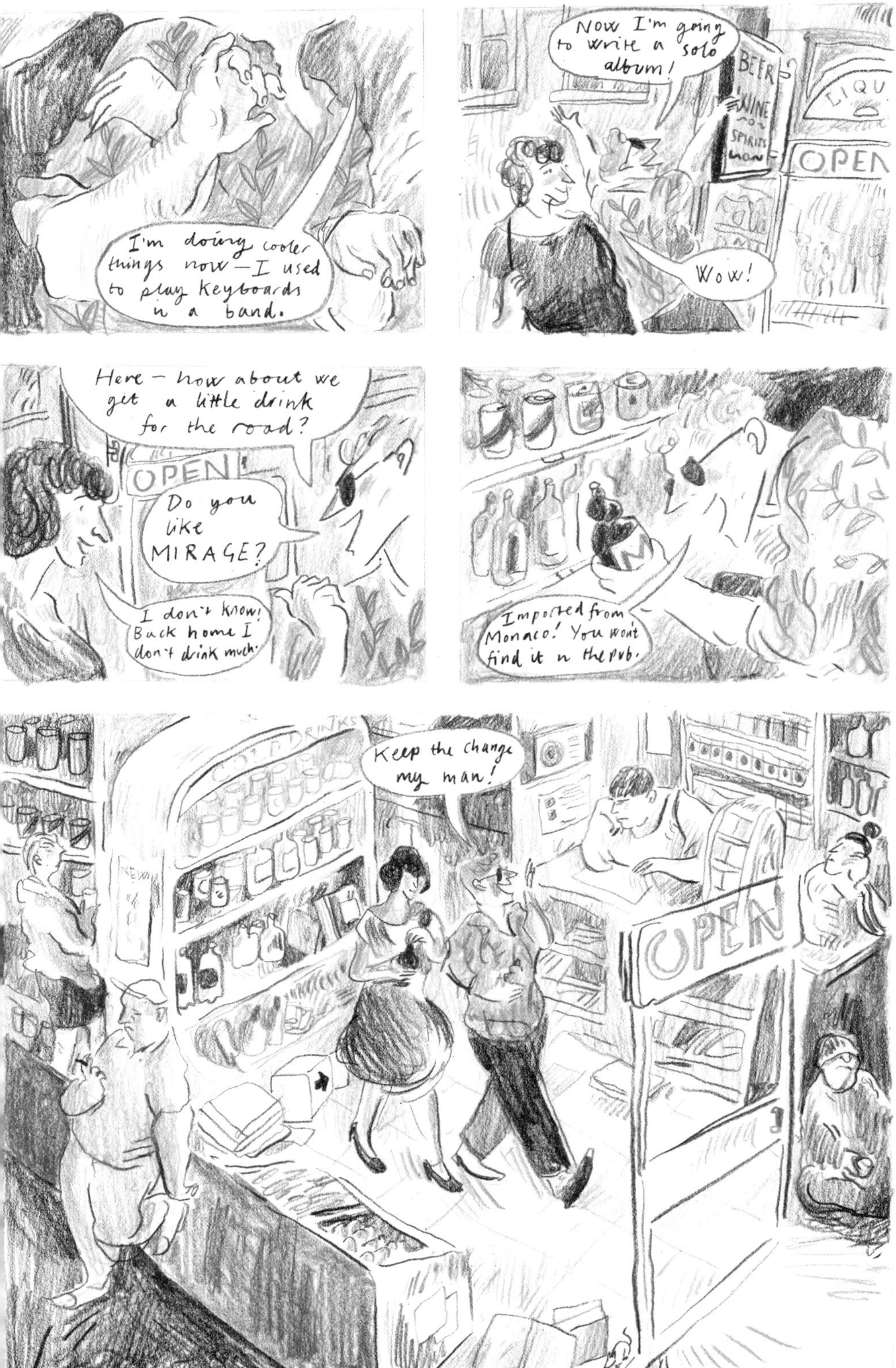
I'm doing cooler things now—I used to play keyboards in a band.
Now I'm going to write a solo album!
BEER WINE SPIRITS
LIQU
OPEN
Wow!
Here—how about we get a little drink for the road?
OPEN
Do you like MIRAGE?
I don't know! Back home I don't drink much.
Imported from Monaco! You won't find it in the pub.
COLD DRINKS
Keep the change my man!
OPEN

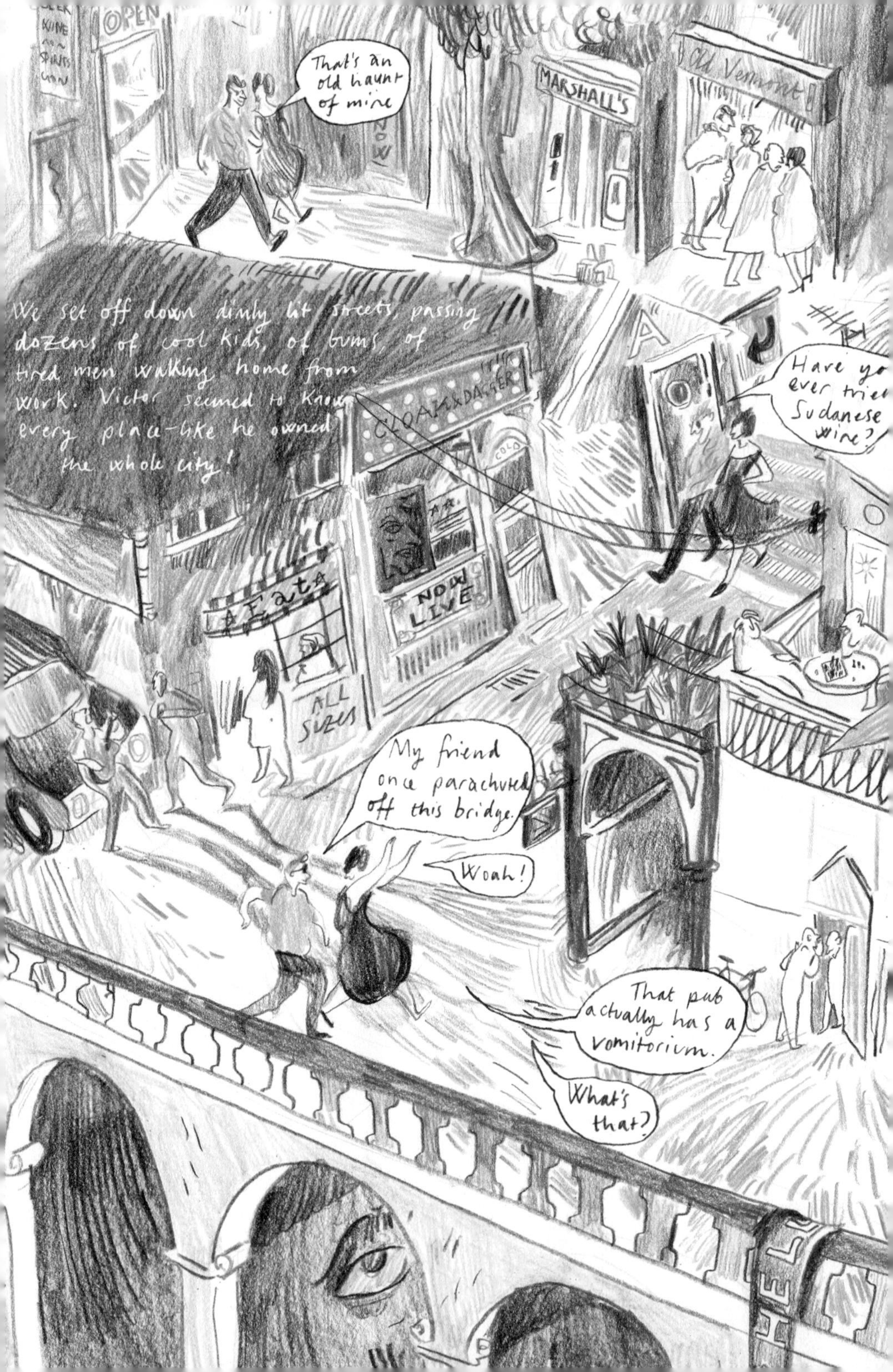
OPEN
MARSHALL'S
Old Vermont
That's an old haunt of mine
We set off down dimly lit streets, passing dozens of cool kids, of bums, of tired men walking home from work. Victor seemed to know every place—like he owned the whole city!
CLOAK&DAGGER
NOW LIVE
ALL SIZES
Have yo ever trie Sudanese wine?
My friend once parachuted off this bridge.
Woah!
That pub actually has a vomitorium.
What's that?

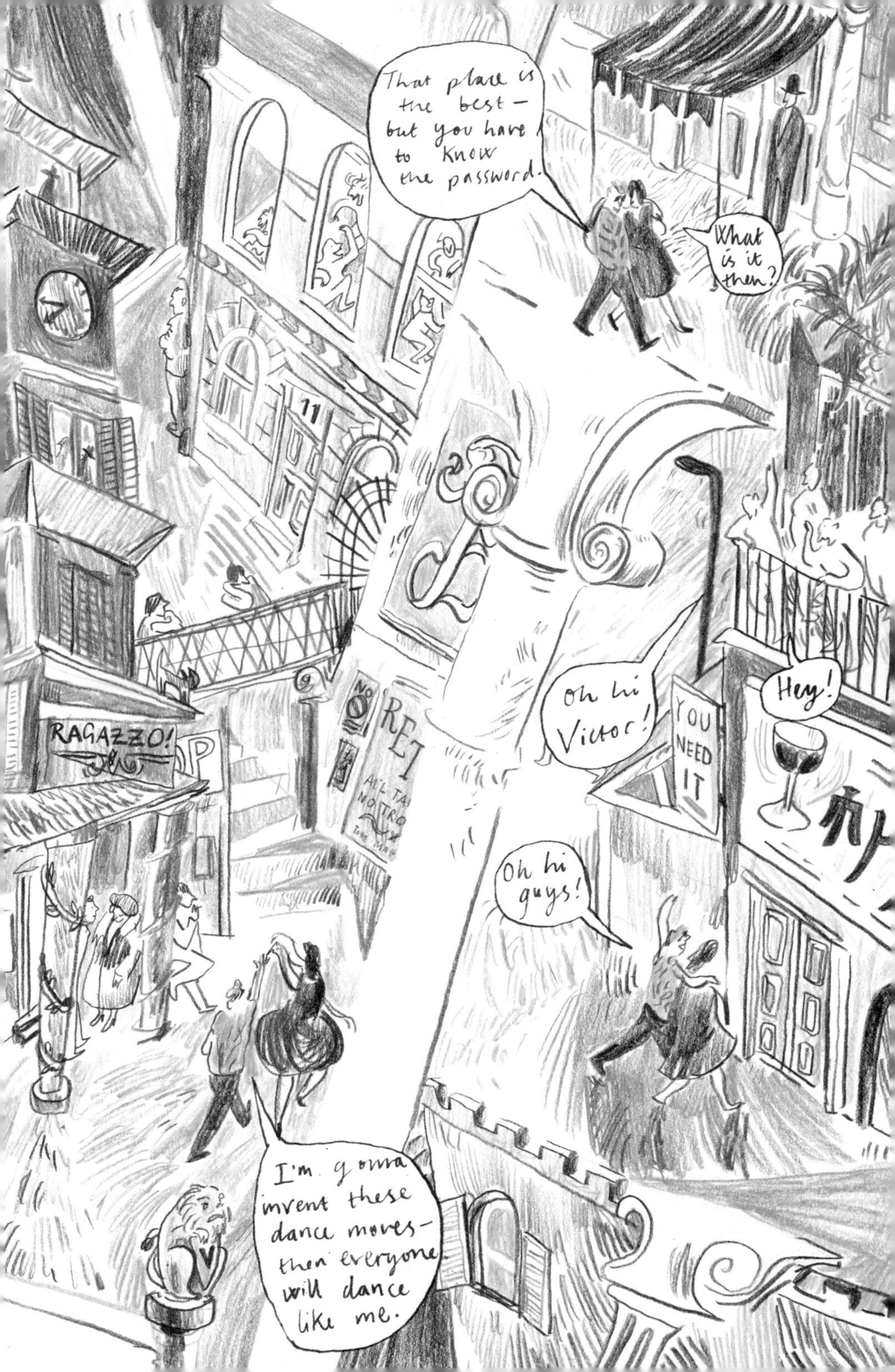
That place is the best— but you have to know the password.
What is it then?
RAGAZZO!
Oh hi Victor!
YOU NEED IT
Hey!
Oh hi guys!
I'm gonna invent these dance moves— then everyone will dance like me.

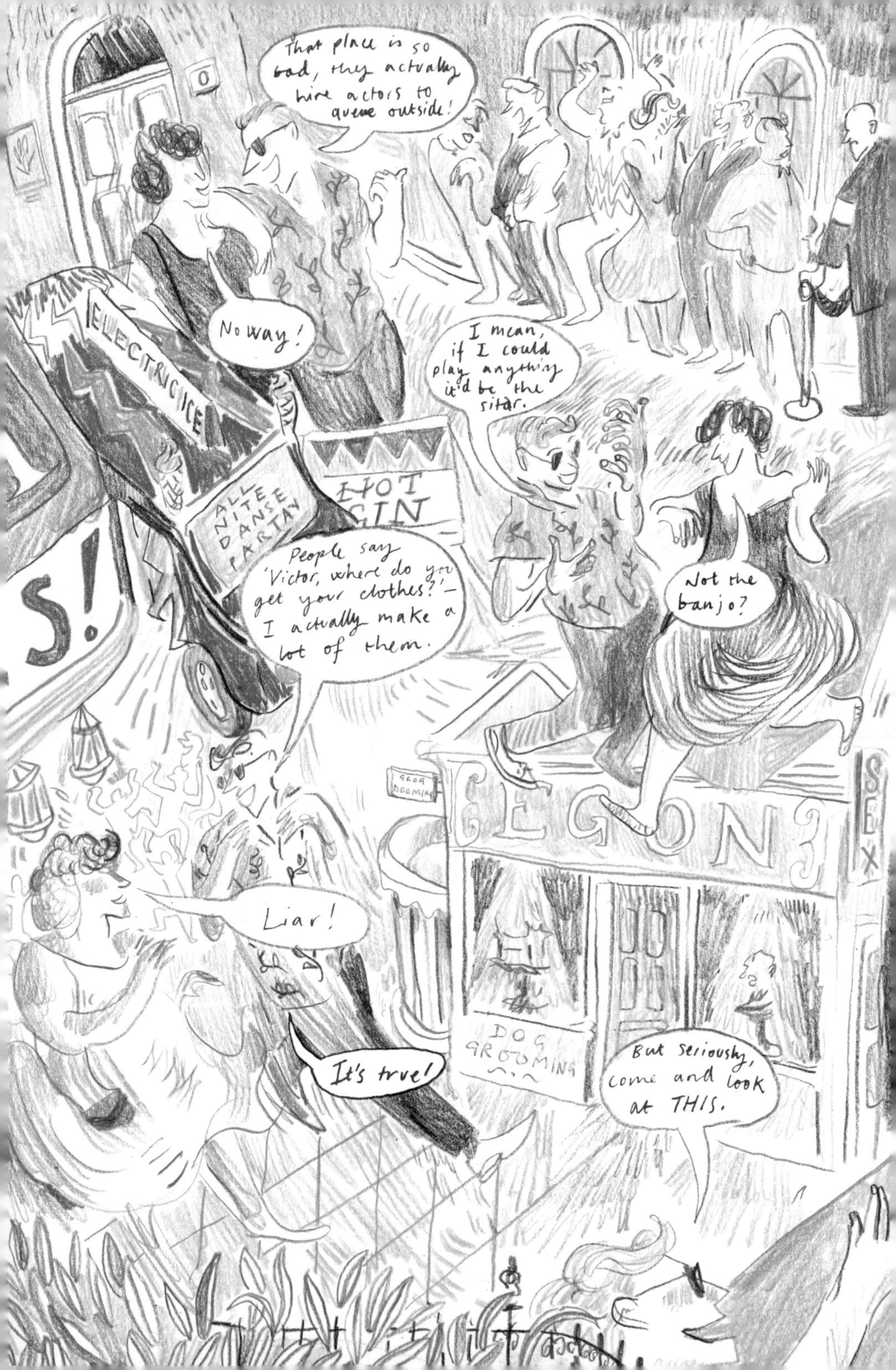
That place is so bad, they actually hire actors to queue outside!
No way!
ELECTRIC ICE
ALL NITE DANSE PARTAY
HOT GIN
I mean, if I could play anything it'd be the sitar.
Not the banjo?
S!
People say 'Victor, where do you get your clothes?' — I actually make a lot of them.
EGON
SEX
Liar!
It's true!
DOG GROOMING
But seriously, come and look at THIS.

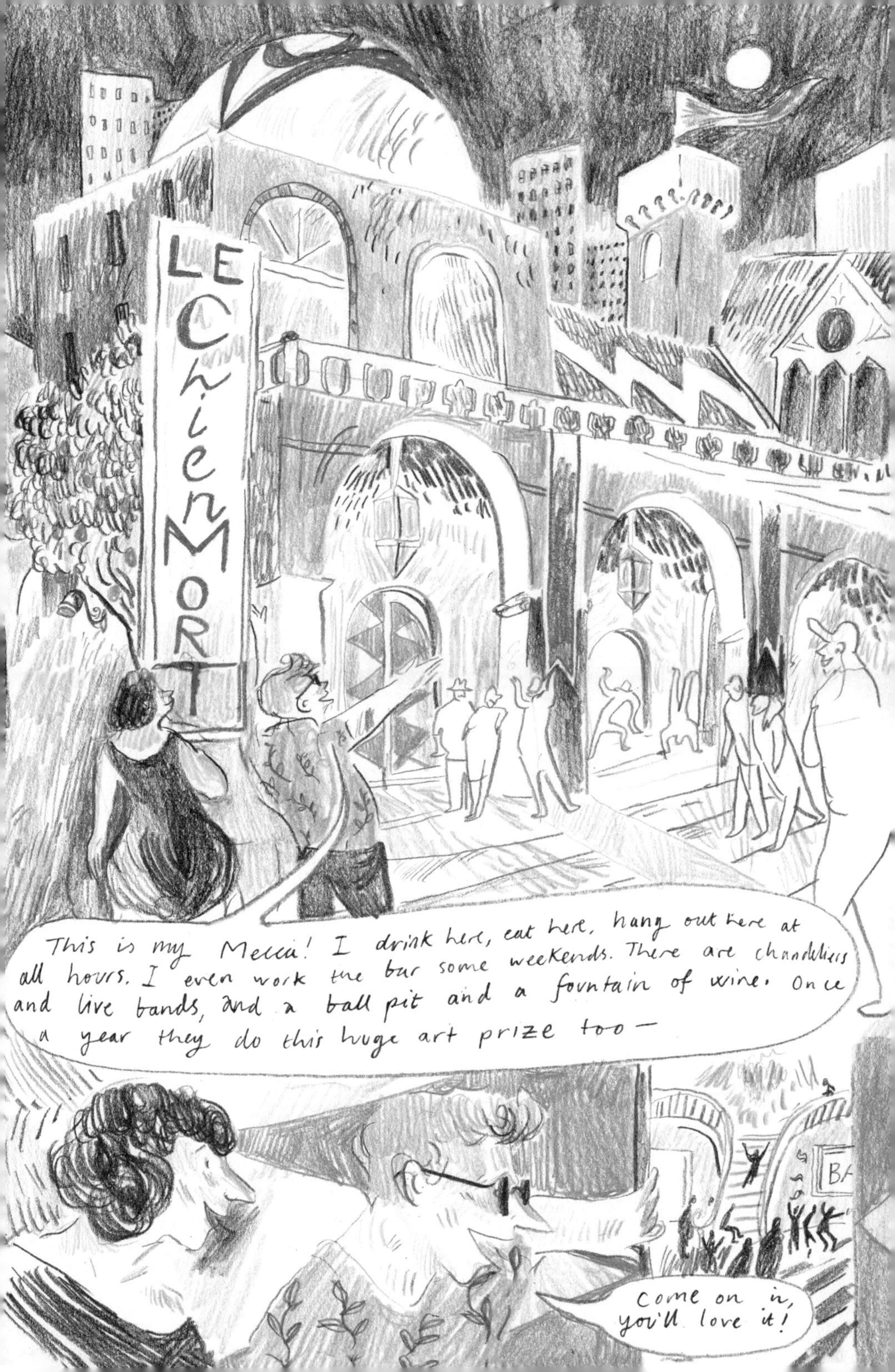
LE Chien MORT
This is my Mecca! I drink here, eat here, hang out here at all hours. I even work the bar some weekends. There are chandeliers and live bands, and a ball pit and a fountain of wine. Once a year they do this huge art prize too—
BA
Come on in, you'll love it!

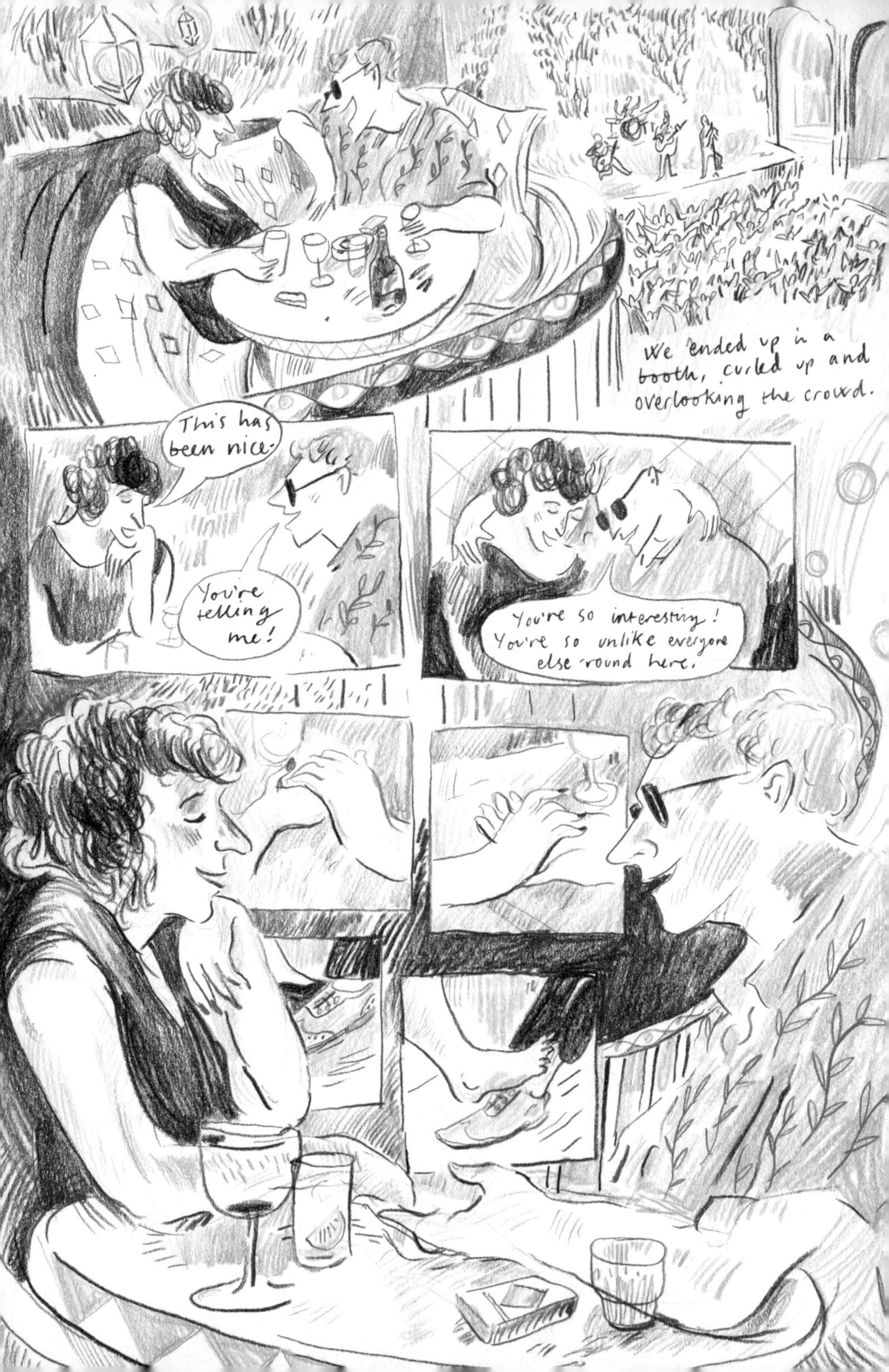

We ended up in a booth, curled up and overlooking the crowd.
This has been nice-
You're telling me!
You're so interesting! You're so unlike everyone else 'round here.

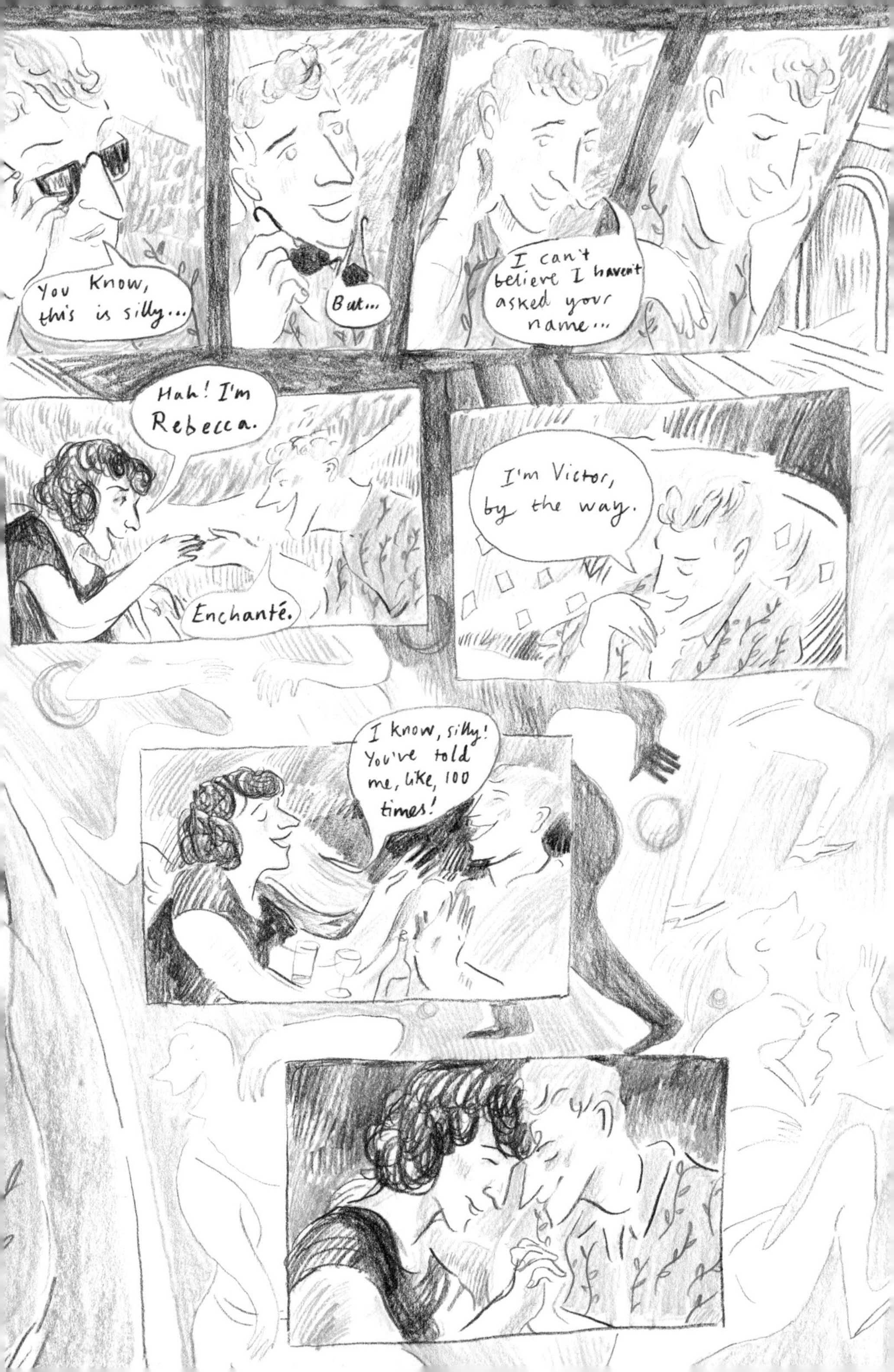
You know, this is silly...
But...
I can't believe I haven't asked your name...
Hah! I'm Rebecca.
Enchanté.
I'm Victor, by the way.
I know, silly! You've told me, like, 100 times!

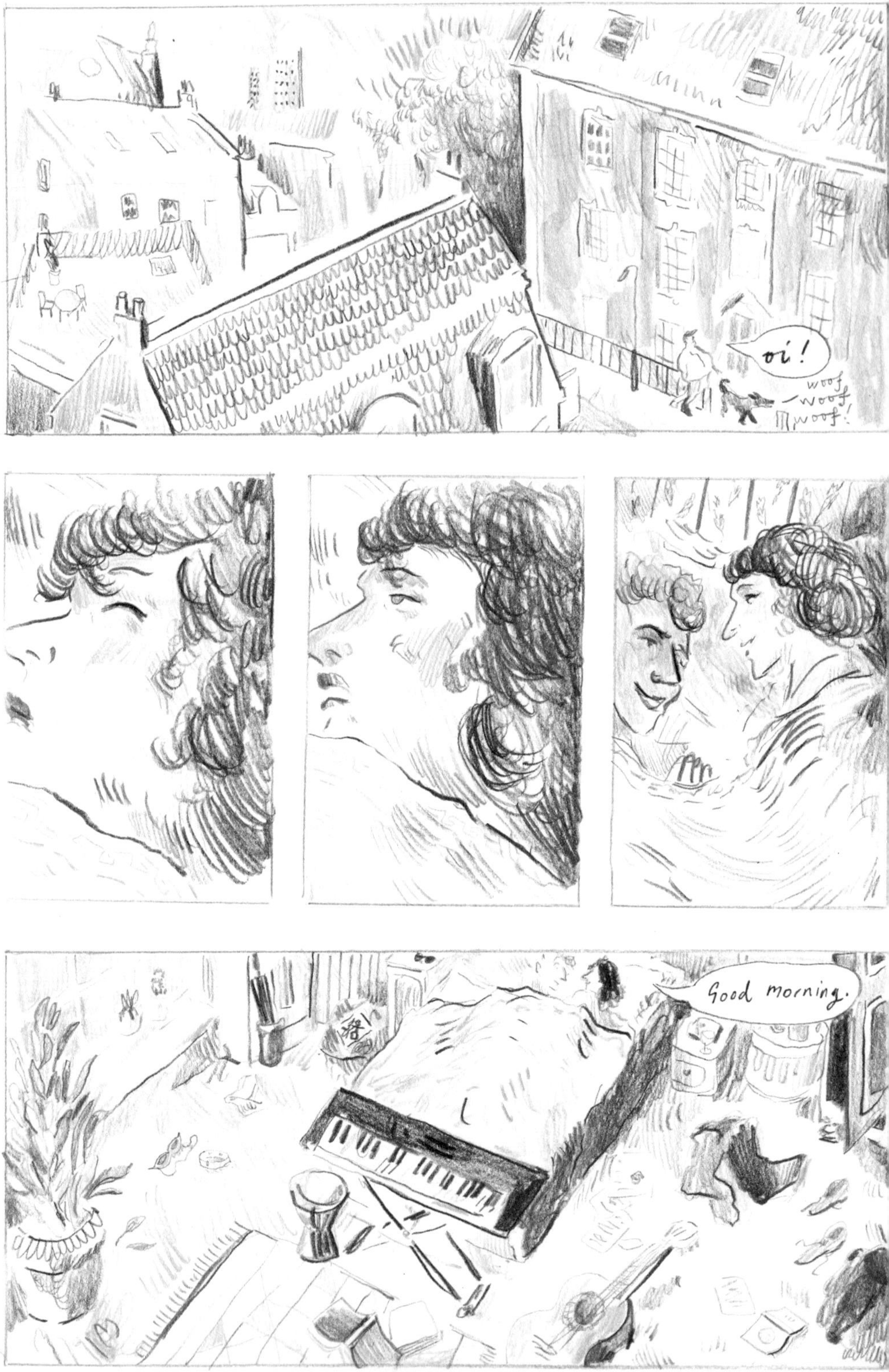
oi!
woof woof woof!
Good morning.

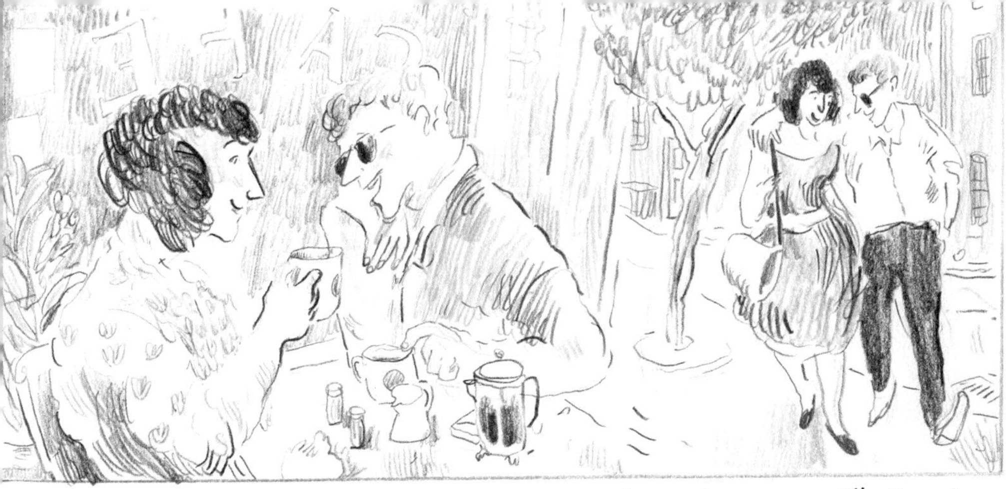

After that, he was so sweet! We started going out all the time.

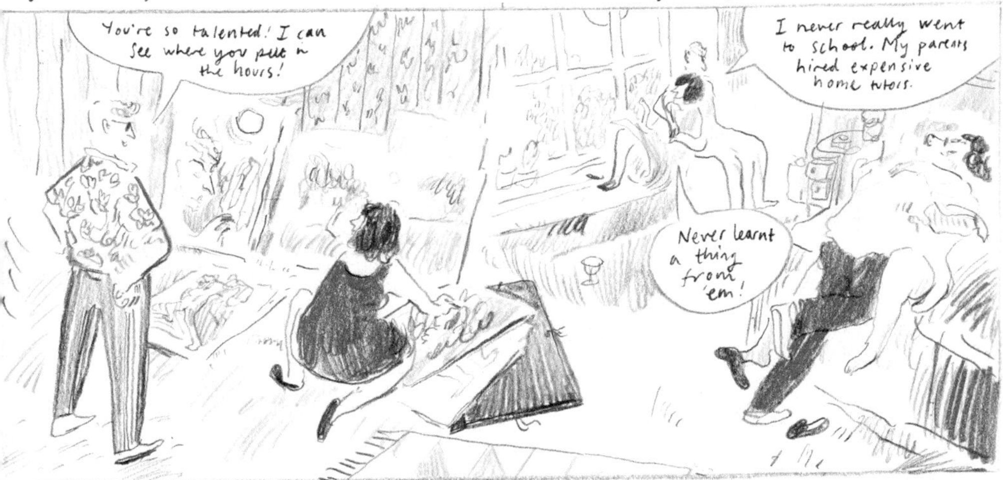
You're so talented! I can see where you put in the hours!
I never really went to school. My parents hired expensive home tutors.
Never learnt a thing from 'em!

We spent ages hanging out in his apartment. I showed him my paintings, he showed off his musical instruments and his collection of giant papier maché heads.— amongst other things.

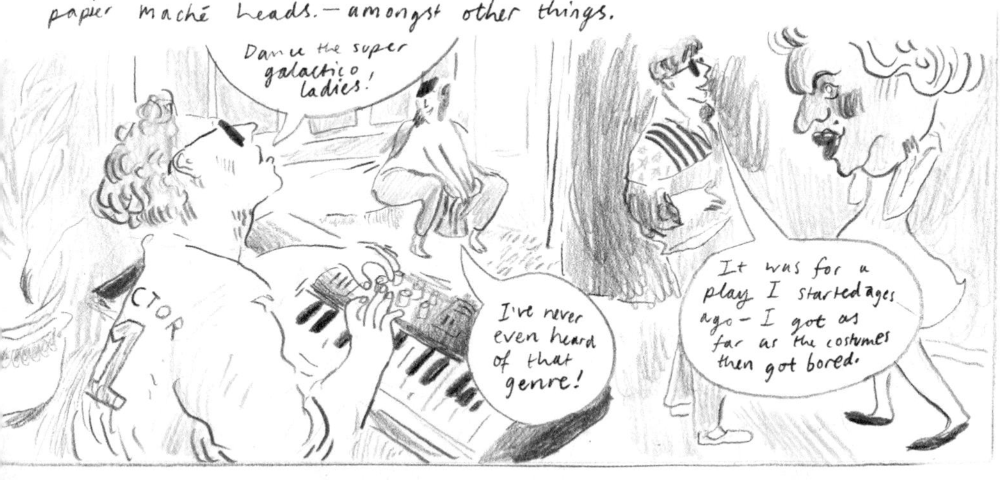
Dance the super galactico ladies!
CTOR
I've never even heard of that genre!
It was for a play I started ages ago— I got as far as the costumes then got bored.

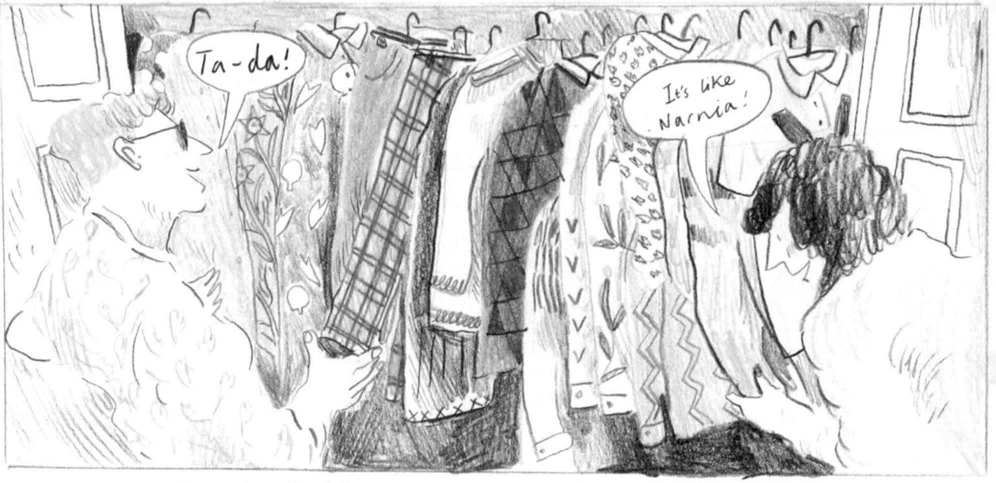
Ta-da!
It's like Narnia!

He showed off his extensive wardrobe.
I showed my terrible guitar playing.
He demonstrated his dreadful cooking.

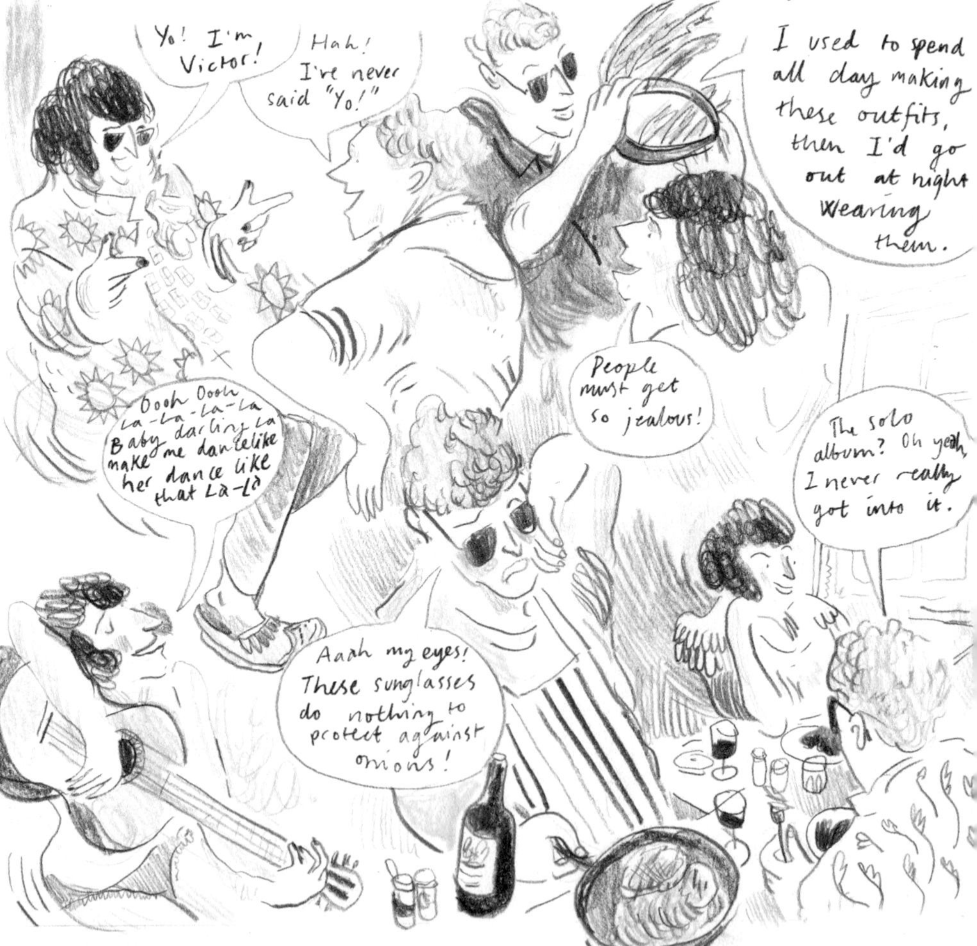
Yo! I'm Victor!
Hah! I've never said "Yo!"
I used to spend all day making these outfits, then I'd go out at night wearing them.
People must get so jealous!
Oooh Oooh La-La-La-La Baby darling La make me dance like her dance like that La-La
The solo album? Oh yeah, I never really got into it.
Aaah my eyes! These sunglasses do nothing to protect against onions!

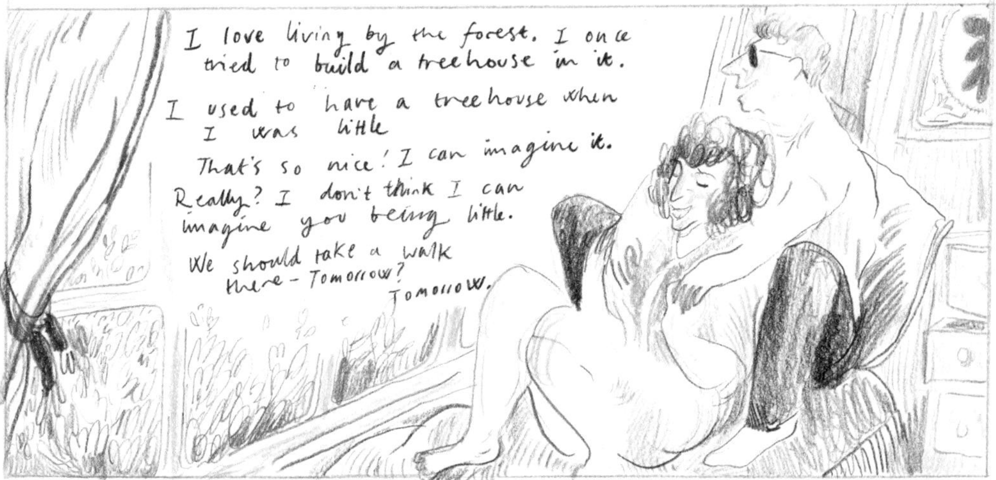
I love living by the forest. I once tried to build a treehouse in it.
I used to have a treehouse when I was little
That's so nice! I can imagine it.
Really? I don't think I can imagine you being little.
We should take a walk there - Tomorrow?
Tomorrow.

Over those weeks we went out dancing dozens of times. I started meeting hundreds of his friends! (Whose names I struggle to remember!)

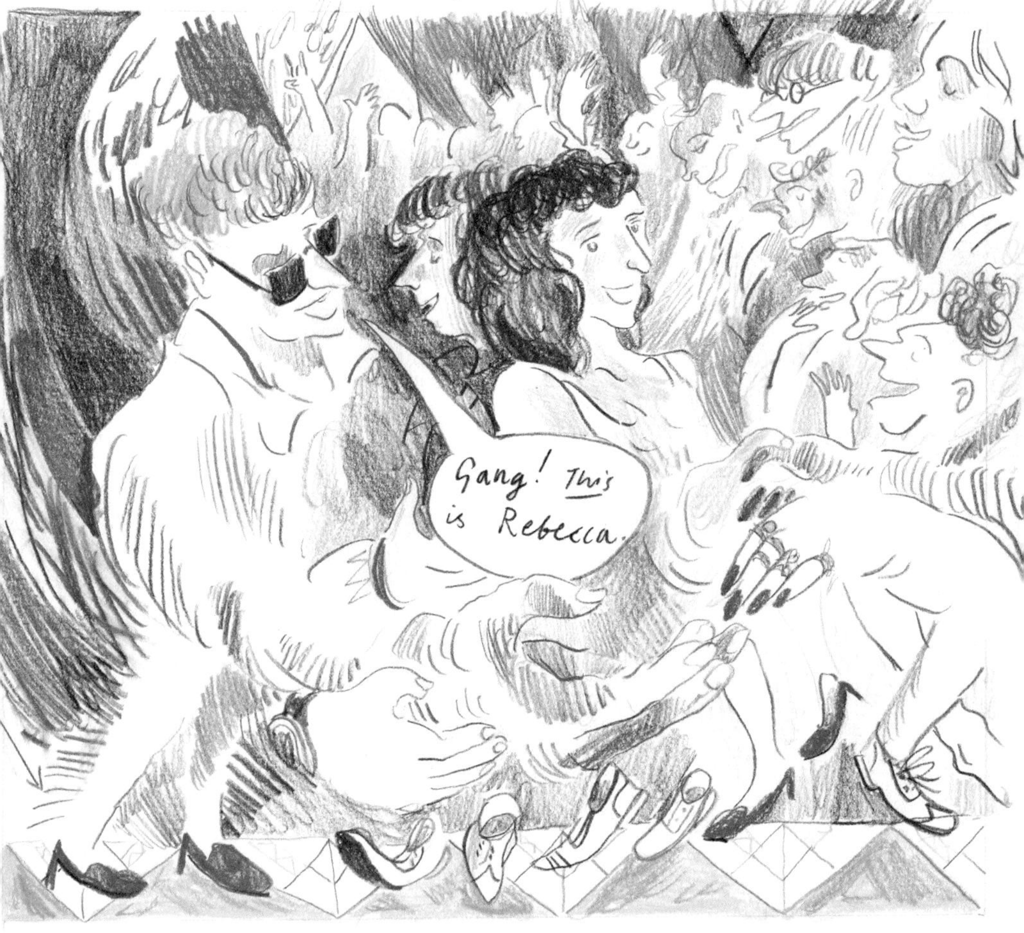
Gang! This is Rebecca.

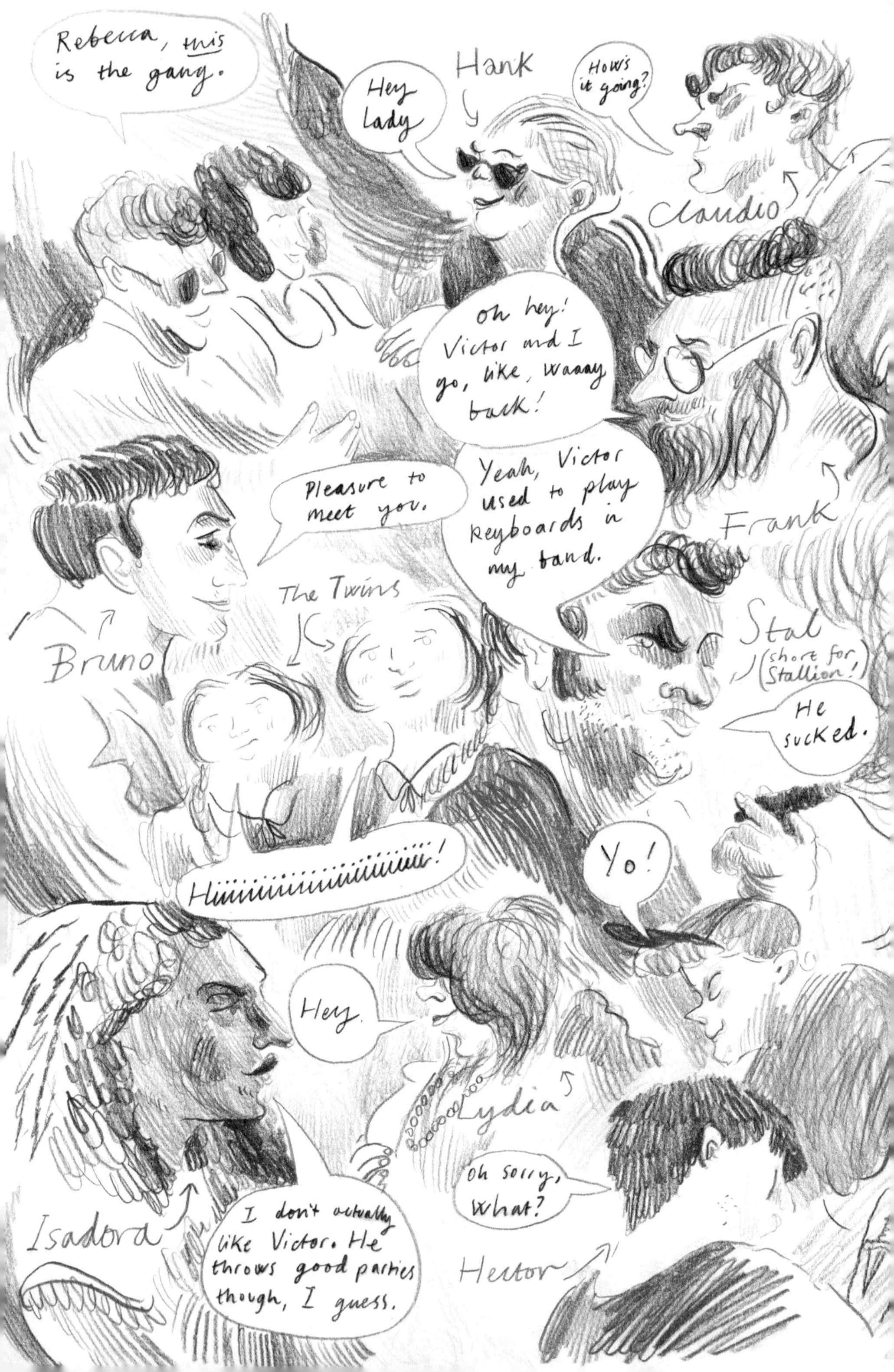
Rebecca, this is the gang.
Hey Lady
Hank
How's it going?
Claudio
Oh hey! Victor and I go, like, waaay back!
Pleasure to meet you.
Yeah, Victor used to play keyboards in my band.
Frank
The Twins
Bruno
Stal (short for Stallion!)
He sucked.
Hiiiiiiiiiiiiiiiiiiiiii!
Yo!
Hey.
Lydia
Oh sorry, what?
Isadora
I don't actually like Victor. He throws good parties though, I guess.
Hector

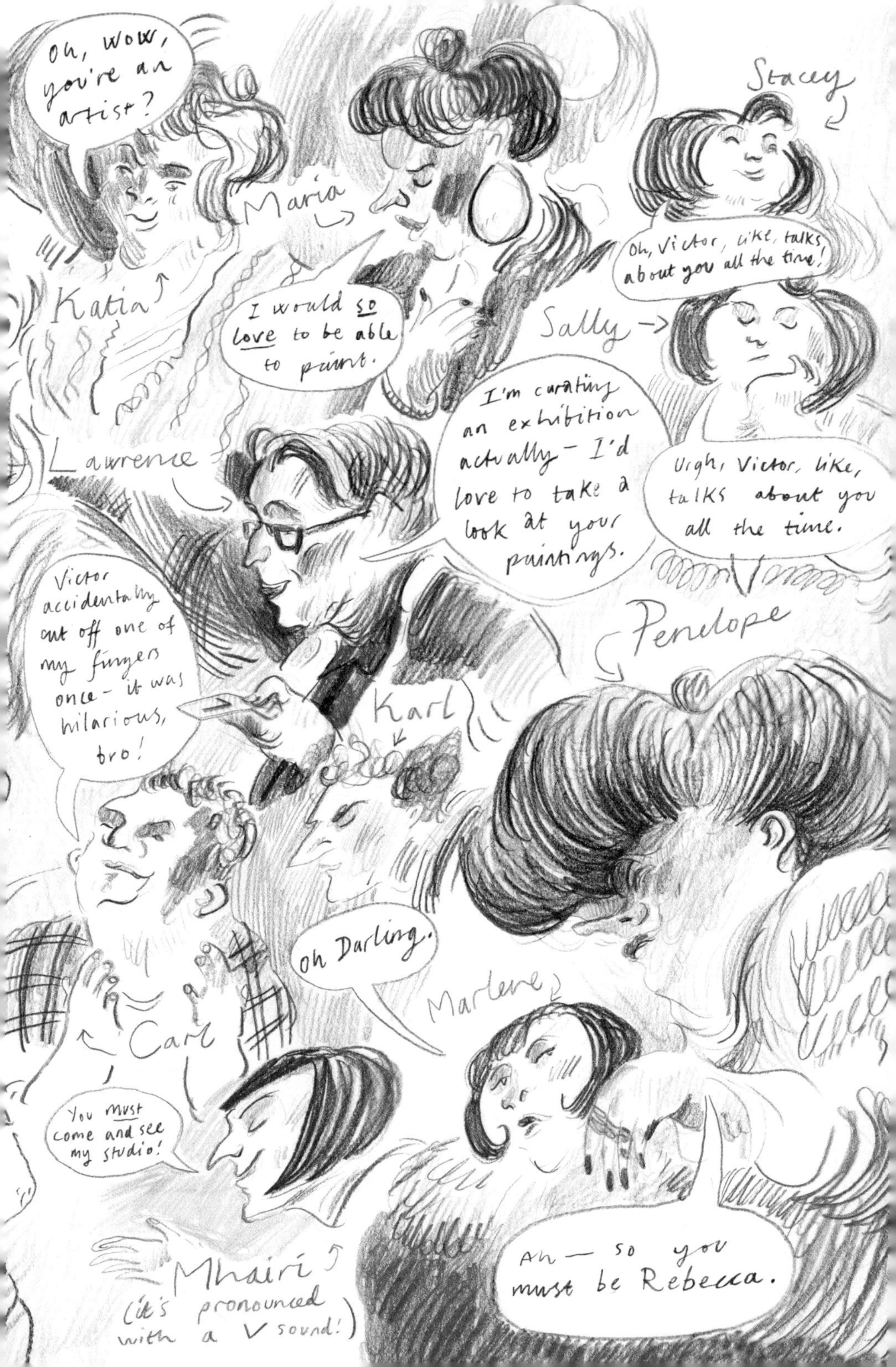
Oh, wow, you're an artist?
Katia
Maria
I would so love to be able to paint.
Stacey
Oh, Victor, like, talks about you all the time!
Sally
I'm curating an exhibition actually - I'd love to take a look at your paintings.
Lawrence
Urgh, Victor, like, talks about you all the time.
Victor accidentally cut off one of my fingers once - it was hilarious, bro!
Penelope
Karl
Oh Darling.
Marlene
Carl
You must come and see my studio!
Mhairi
(it's pronounced with a V sound!)
Ah - so you must be Rebecca.

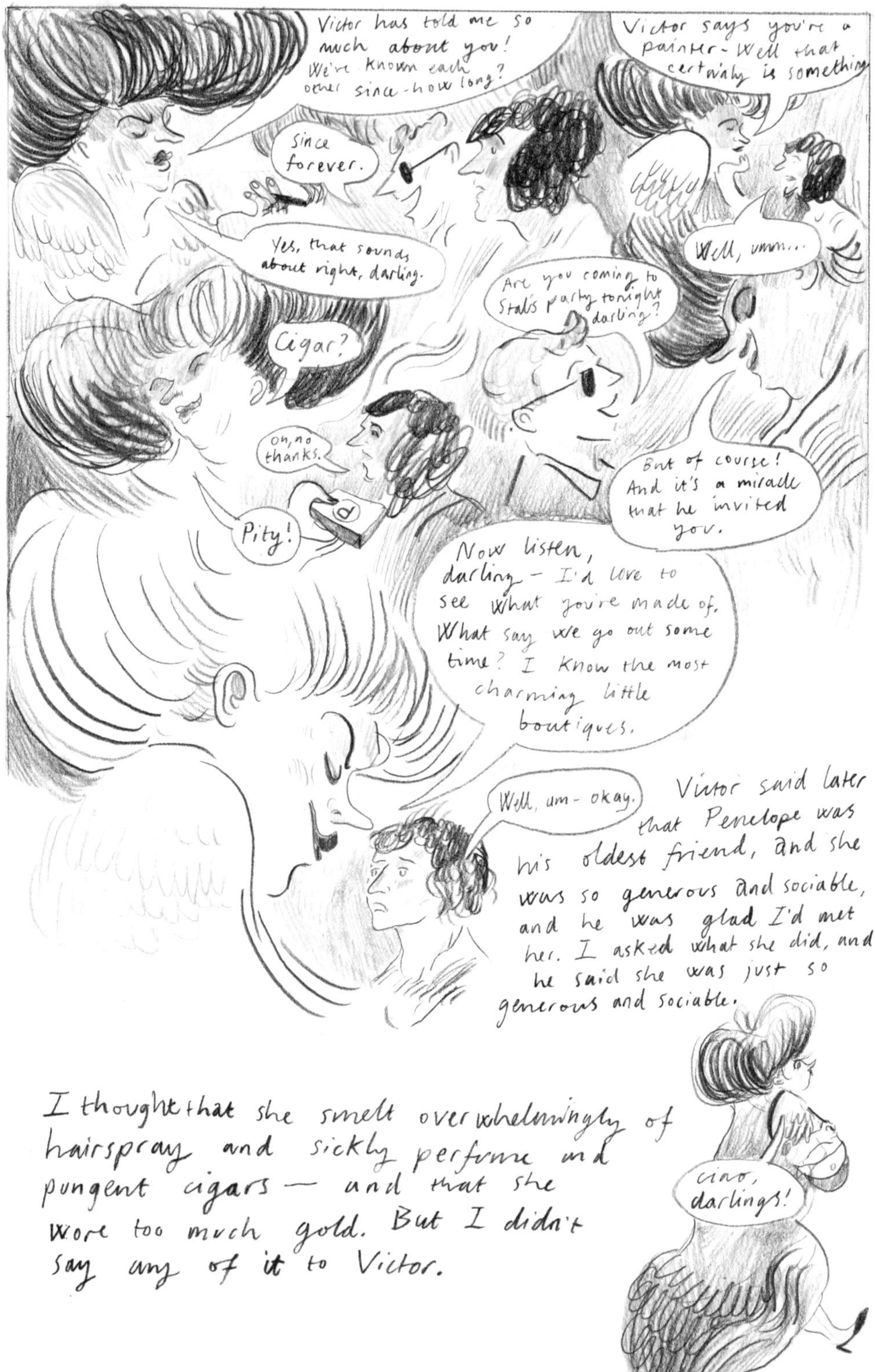
Victor has told me so much about you! We've known each other since- how long?
since forever.
Yes, that sounds about right, darling.
Victor says you're a painter- Well that certainly is something
Well, umm...
Are you coming to Stal's party tonight darling?
Cigar?
Oh, no thanks.
Pity!
But of course! And it's a miracle that he invited you.
Now listen, darling - I'd love to see what you're made of. What say we go out some time? I know the most charming little boutiques.
Well, um- okay.
Victor said later that Penelope was his oldest friend, and she was so generous and sociable, and he was glad I'd met her. I asked what she did, and he said she was just so generous and sociable.
I thought that she smelt overwhelmingly of hairspray and sickly perfume and pungent cigars — and that she wore too much gold. But I didn't say any of it to Victor.
ciao, darlings!

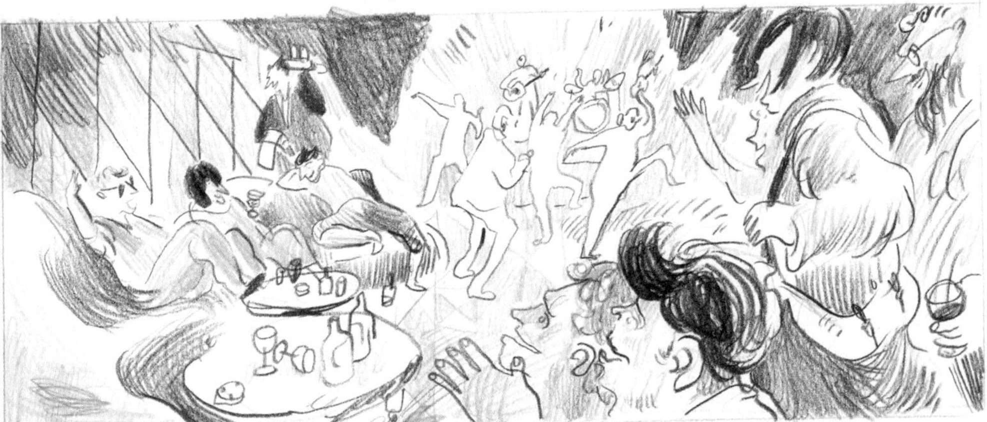

The weeks descended into a haze of dances and parties and everyone liked me, and told me so. It's such a thrill to go into a room full of people, where everyone wants to be around you!

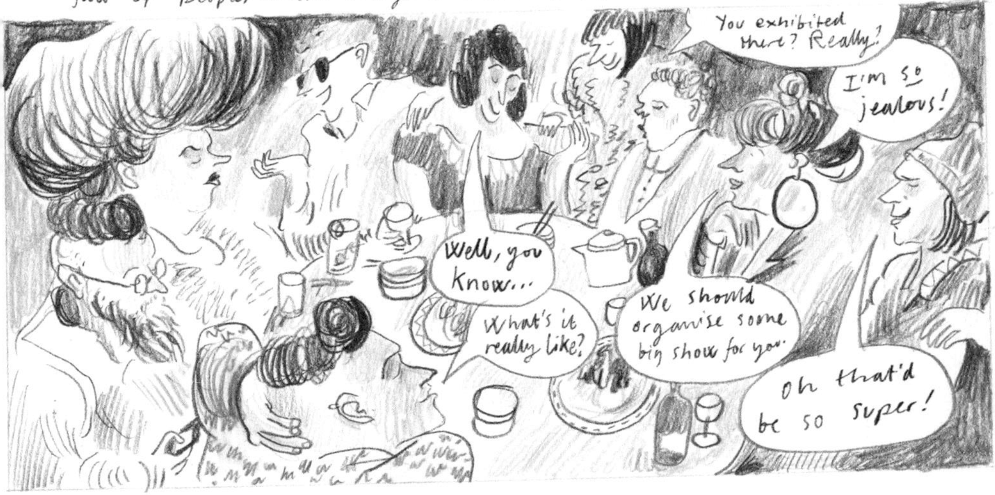

You exhibited there? Really!
I'm so jealous!
Well, you know...
What's it really like?
We should organise some big show for you.
Oh that'd be so super!

Victor wanted to spend every minute with me - it was BLISS!

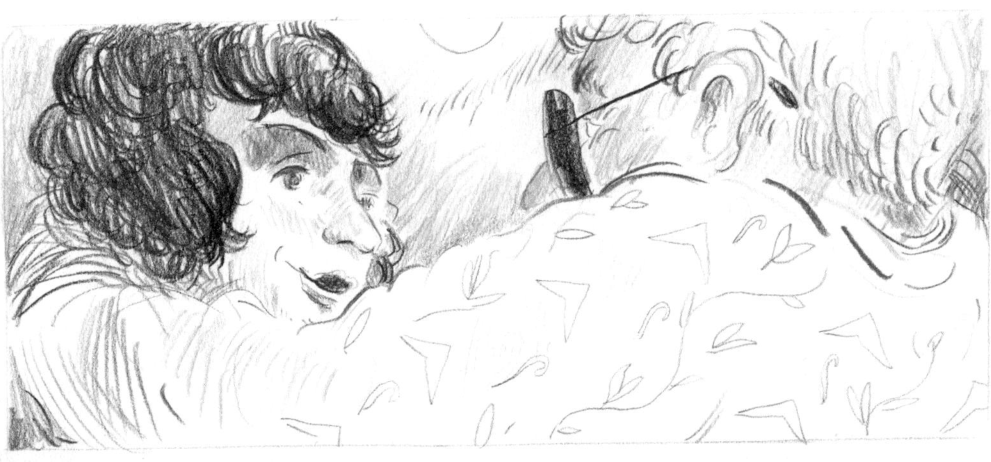

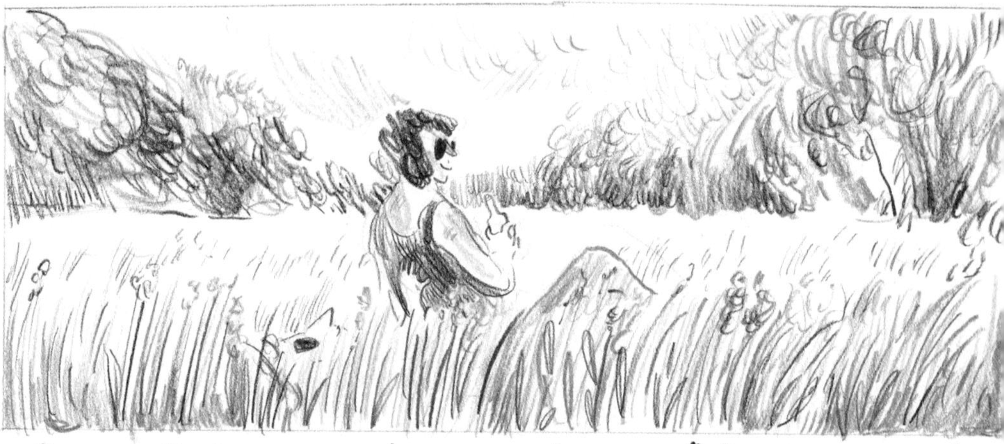

One weekend we borrowed a car and went off to the countryside.
His friend Mhairi invited me to share her studio —
so I had somewhere to paint again!

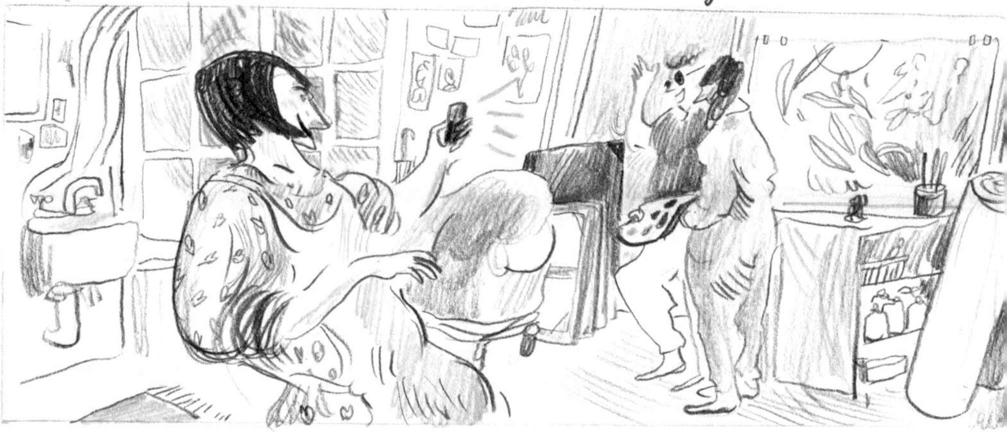

And when I finally got sick of my cousin's attic, Victor
invited me to move in with him.

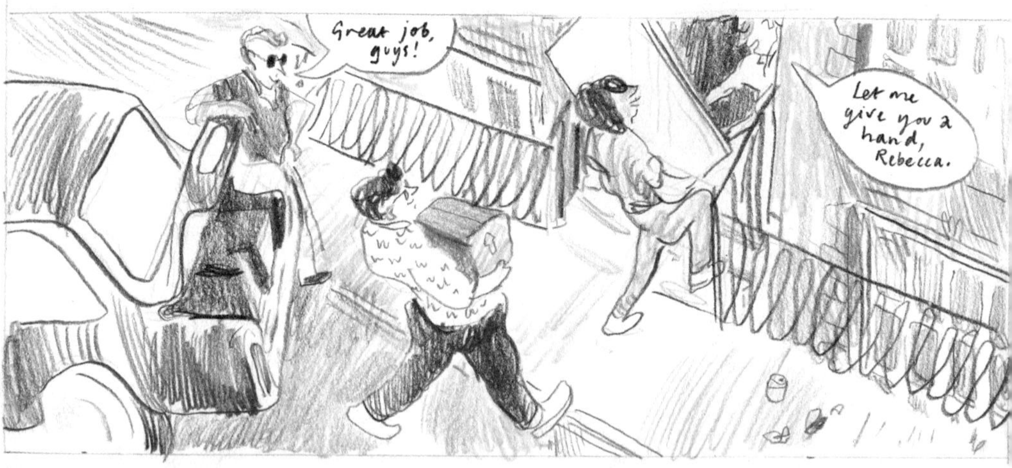
Great job, guys!
Let me give you a hand, Rebecca.

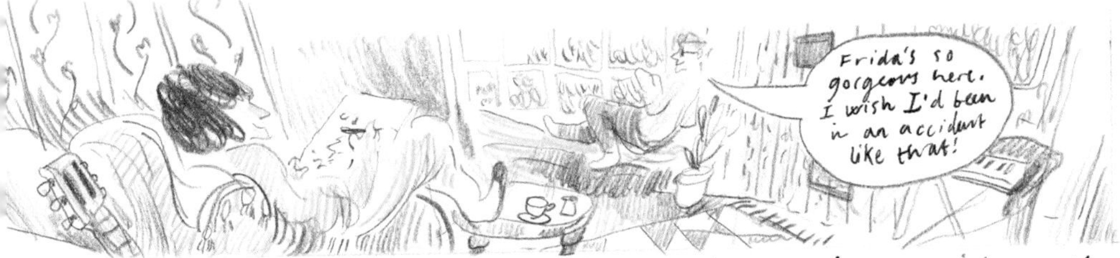
Frida's so gorgeous here. I wish I'd been in an accident like that!

We spent all day lying around together, and all night out drinking and dancing – like I said: BLISS!

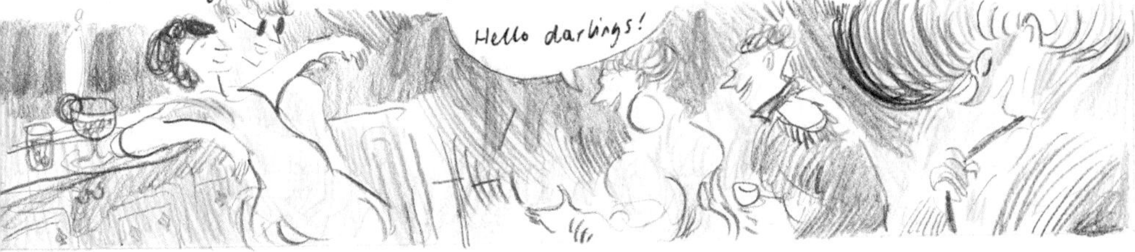
Hello darlings!

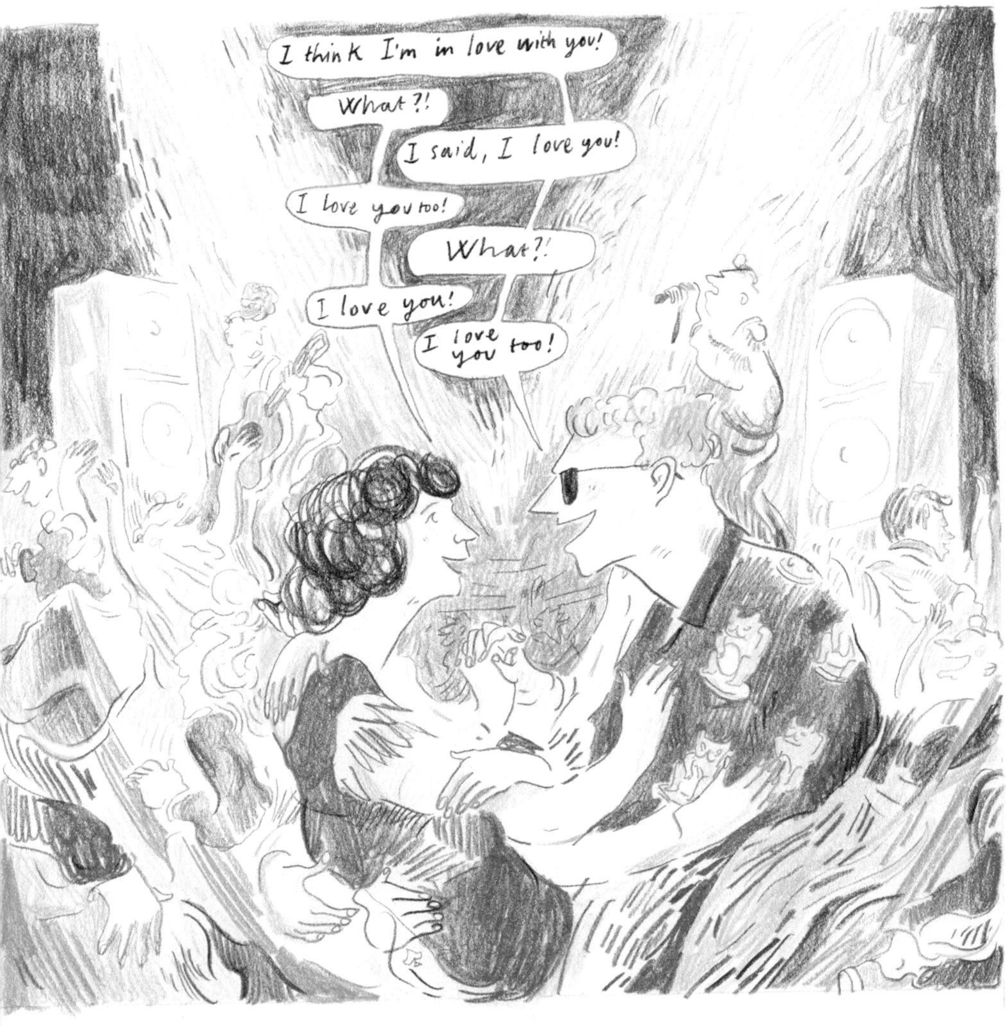
I think I'm in love with you!
What?!
I said, I love you!
I love you too!
What?!
I love you!
I love you too!

The months flew by. I settled into Victor's flat, I had a studio, I was living the good life. We were the most popular couple around! True to his word, Victor's friend Lawrence had got four of my paintings into a group exhibition in a fashionable gallery.

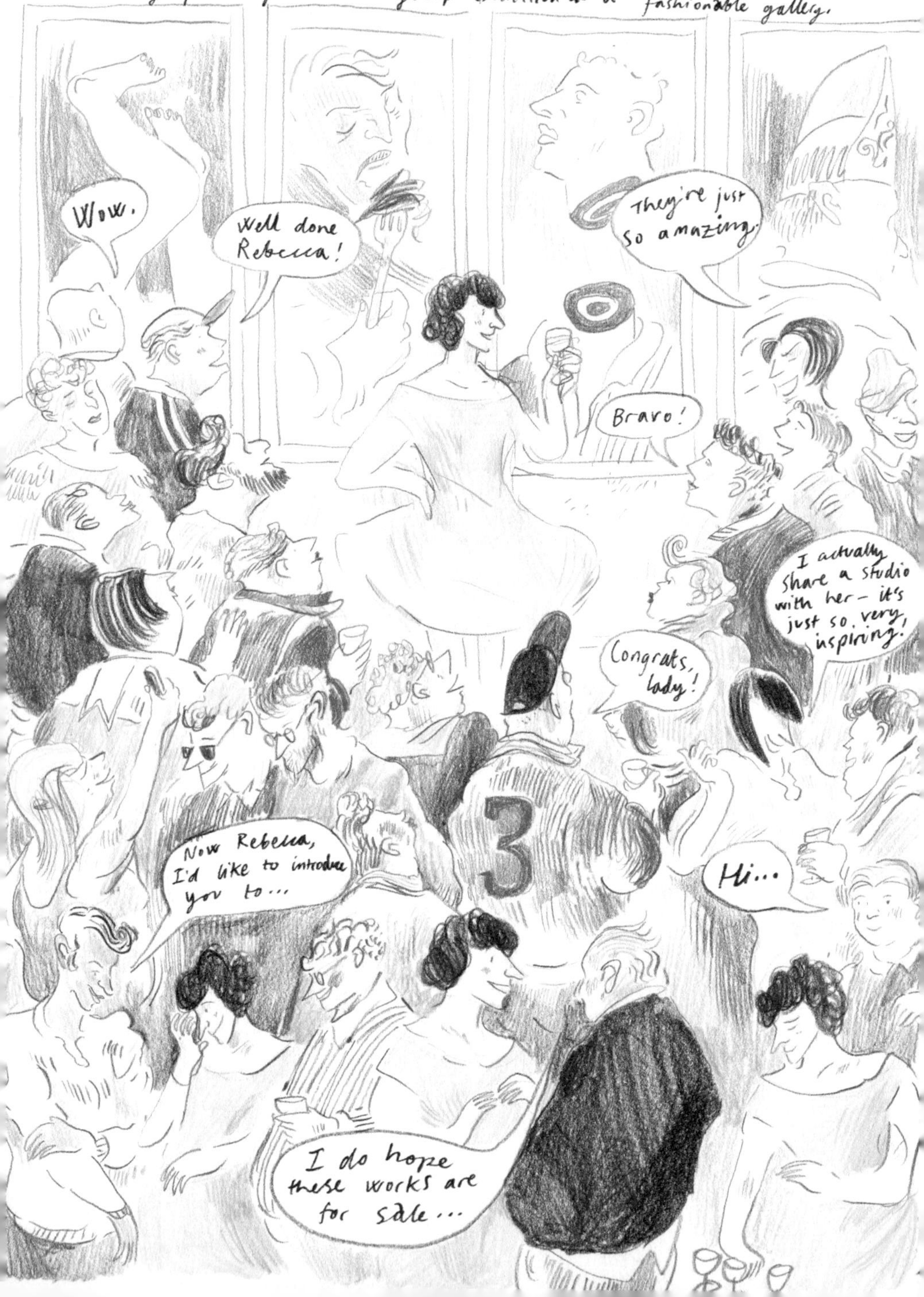
Wow.
Well done Rebecca!
They're just so amazing.
Bravo!
I actually share a studio with her – it's just so, very, inspiring.
Congrats, lady!
Now Rebecca, I'd like to introduce you to...
Hi...
I do hope these works are for sale...

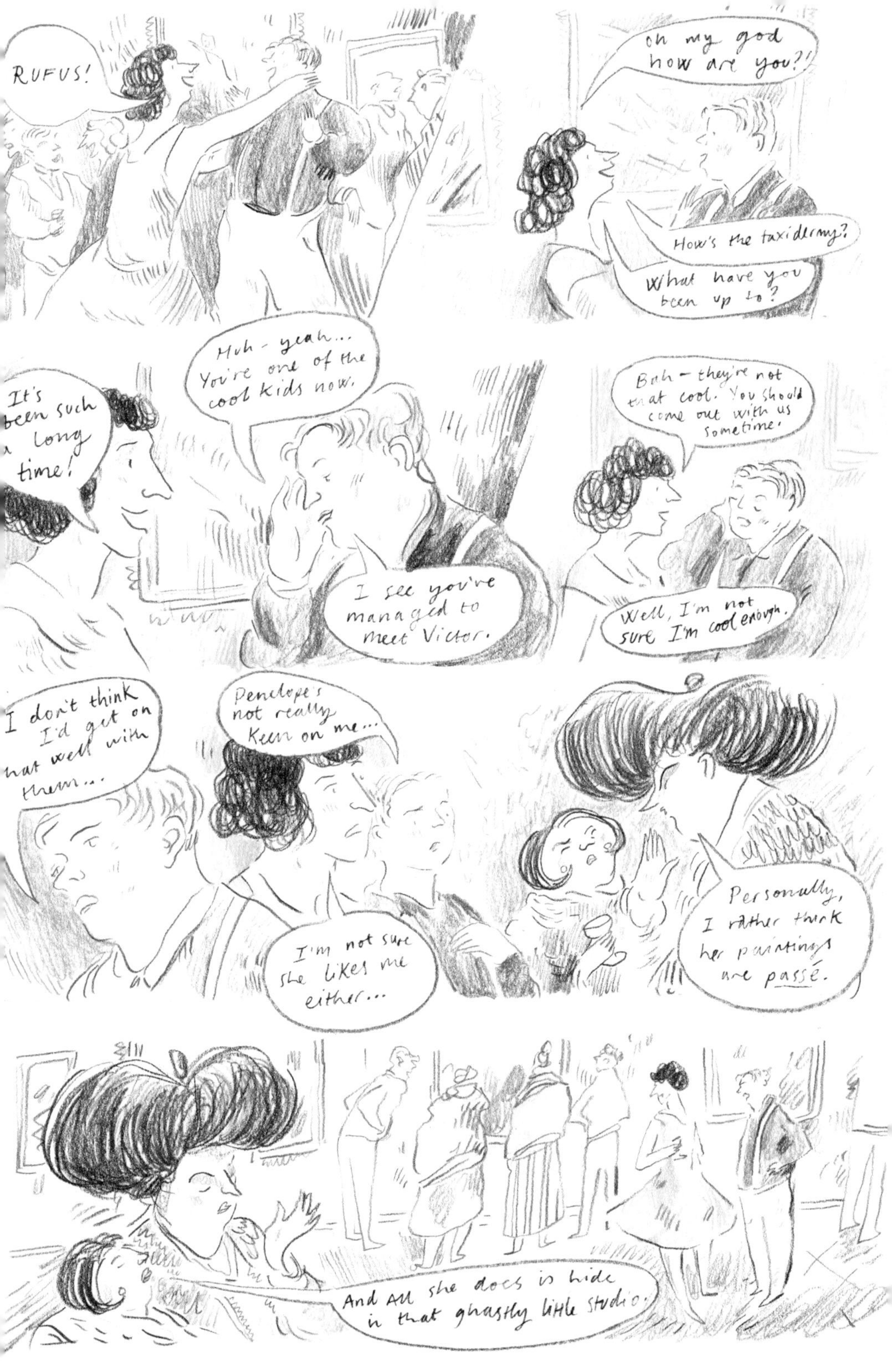
RUFUS!
Oh my god how are you?!
How's the taxidermy?
What have you been up to?
It's been such a long time!
Huh - yeah... You're one of the cool kids now.
I see you've managed to meet Victor.
Bah - they're not that cool. You should come out with us sometime.
Well, I'm not sure I'm cool enough.
I don't think I'd get on that well with them...
Penelope's not really keen on me...
I'm not sure she likes me either...
Personally, I rather think her paintings are passé.
And all she does is hide in that ghastly little studio.

Still – everyone else seemed to enjoy the exhibition. Rufus had made more terrifying taxidermy sculptures (explaining "Yes, I use found roadkill, mostly"!), while Lawrence had produced a series of etchings too small to actually see, and Frank had built a large cupboard in which a computer read out tiresome poetry over the deafening sound of birdsong.

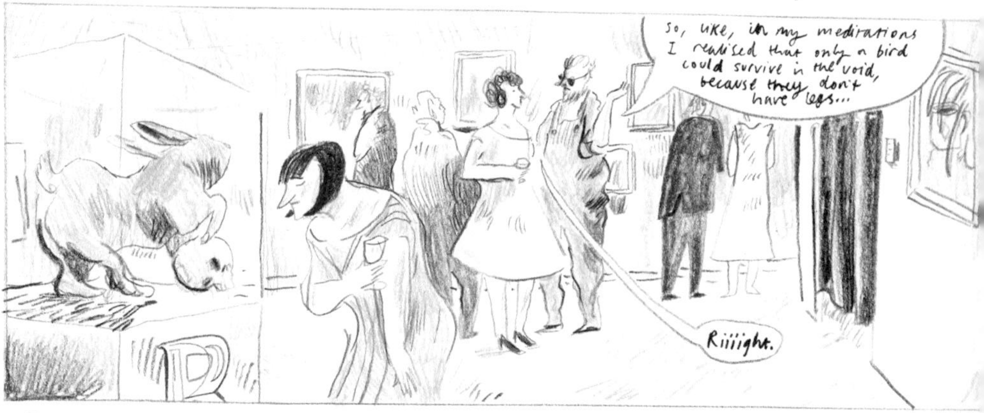
So, like, in my meditations I realised that only a bird could survive in the void, because they don't have legs...
Riiiight.

Victor looked at my paintings for a while and said "Yeah great job", then drifted around the gallery. He didn't say anything else about them. Not that I really, like, care though, because loads of other people complimented them, and I even sold one, so if Victor wants to be all cool and aloof then I'll just let him...

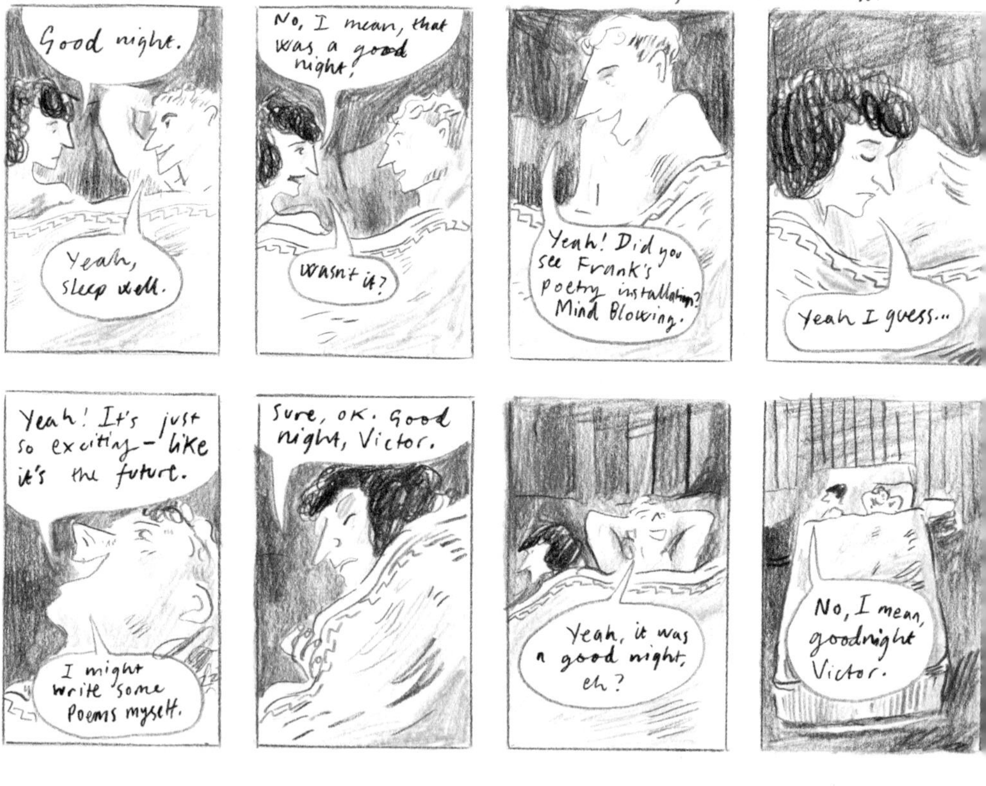
Good night.
Yeah, sleep well.
No, I mean, that was a good night!
Wasn't it?
Yeah! Did you see Frank's poetry installation? Mind Blowing.
Yeah I guess...
Yeah! It's just so exciting – like it's the future.
I might write some Poems myself.
Sure, OK. Good night, Victor.
Yeah, it was a good night, eh?
No, I mean, goodnight Victor.

sulked for most of the following day, until Victor took me out
dinner, then I felt better. Plus, we ran into Lawrence, who
aid I'd sold another painting, so that made everything perfect.

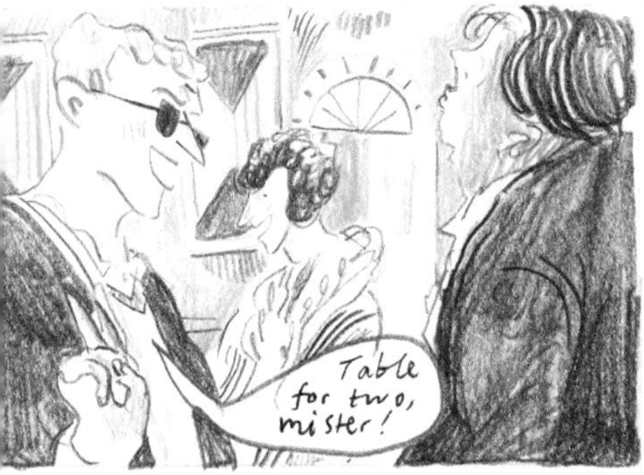
Table for two, mister!

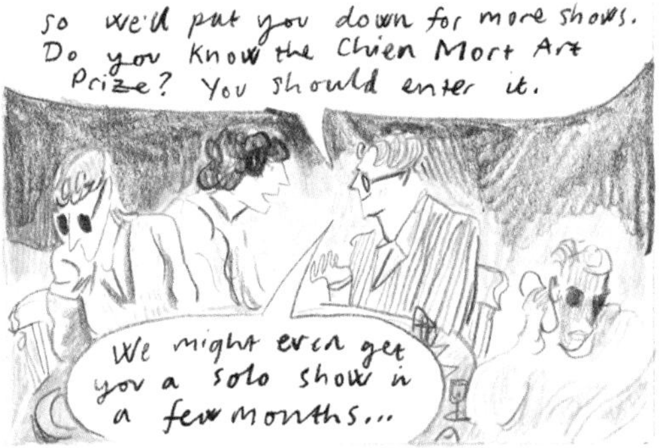
So we'll put you down for more shows. Do you know the Chien Mort Art Prize? You should enter it.
We might even get you a solo show in a few months...

To his credit, Victor seemed serious about writing poetry. He
repurposed his keyboard as a desk, and when some of his
followers said they didn't entirely "get it," he branded them
"uncool" and found some new, real poet friends.

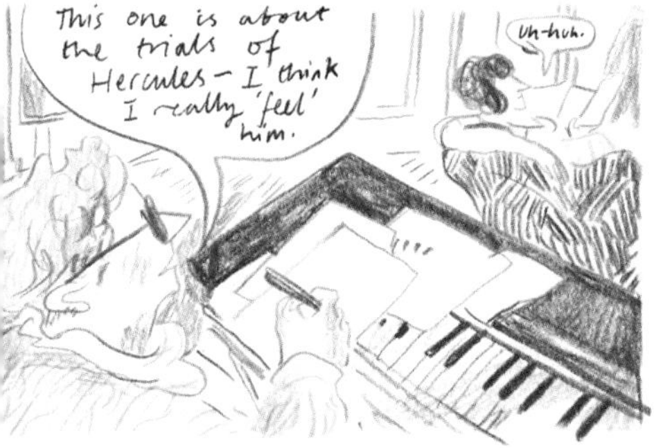
This one is about the trials of Hercules – I think I really 'feel' him.
Uh-huh.

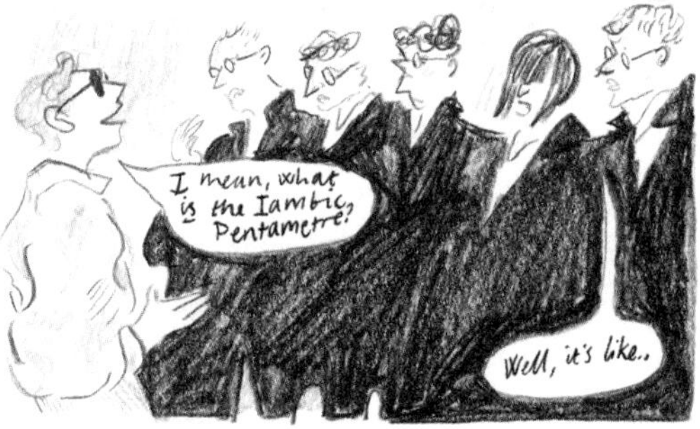
I mean, what is the Iambic Pentametre?
Well, it's like..

lot that I minded, because it gave me more time in the studio, and I
ould hang out with my own friends more. Although it would
ave been nice if he'd found other things to talk about...

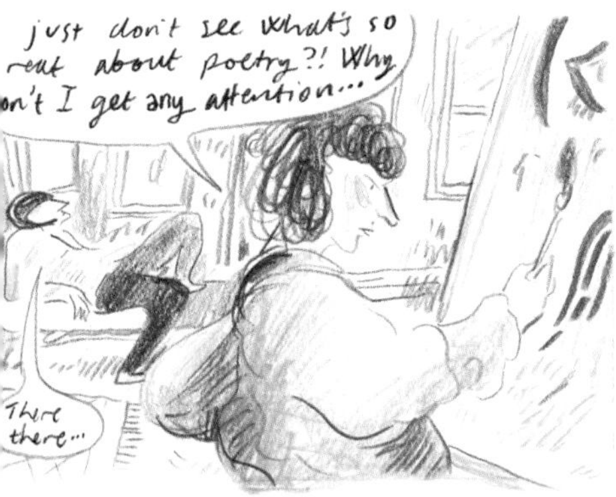
just don't see what's so reat about poetry?! Why on't I get any attention...
There there...

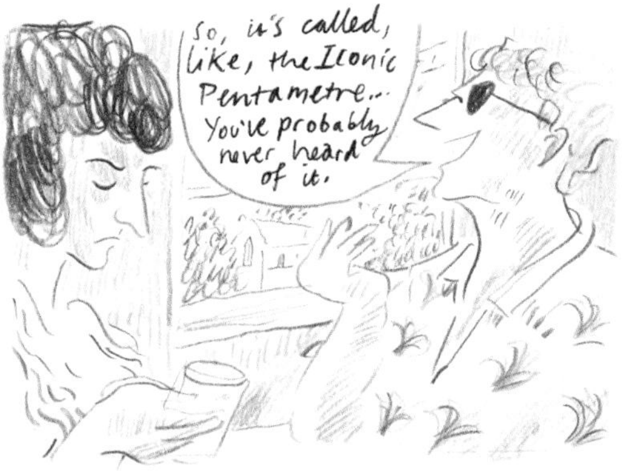
So, it's called, like, the Iconic Pentametre... You've probably never heard of it.

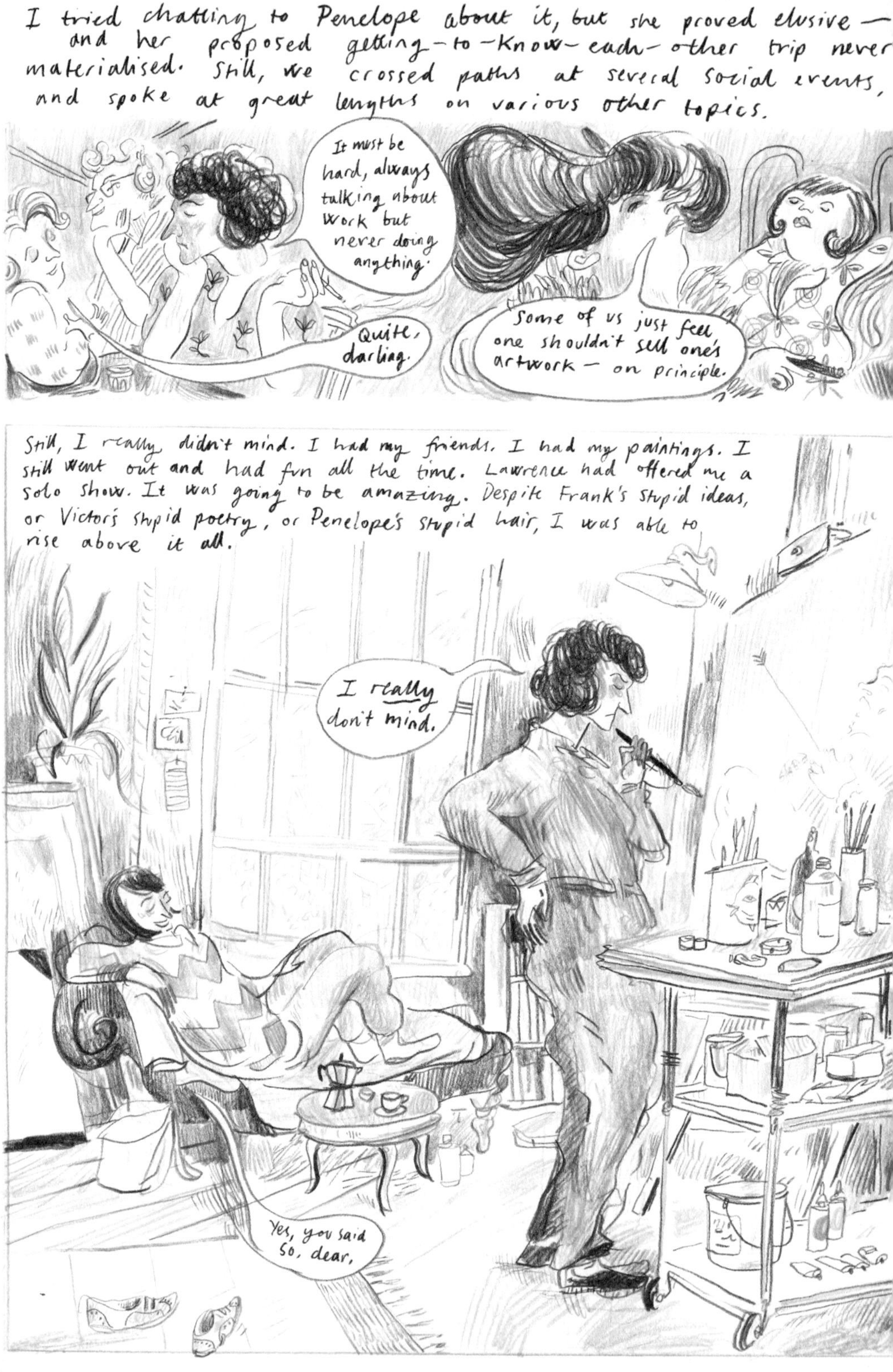
I tried chatting to Penelope about it, but she proved elusive — and her proposed getting-to-know-each-other trip never materialised. Still, we crossed paths at several social events, and spoke at great lengths on various other topics.
It must be hard, always talking about work but never doing anything.
Quite, darling.
Some of us just feel one shouldn't sell one's artwork — on principle.
Still, I really didn't mind. I had my friends. I had my paintings. I still went out and had fun all the time. Lawrence had offered me a solo show. It was going to be amazing. Despite Frank's stupid ideas, or Victor's stupid poetry, or Penelope's stupid hair, I was able to rise above it all.
I really don't mind.
Yes, you said so, dear.

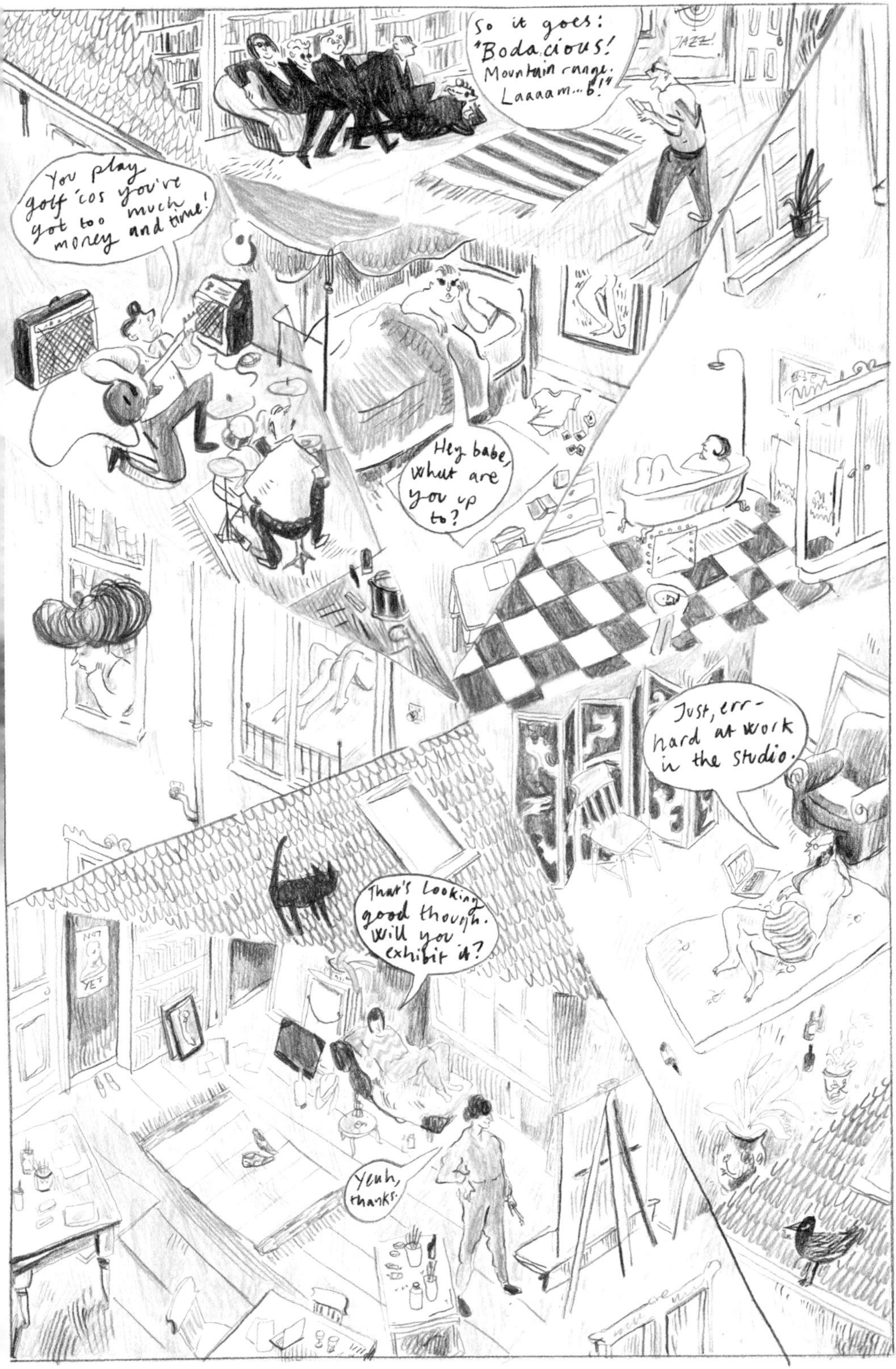
So it goes: "Bodacious! Mountain range. Laaaam...b!"
You play golf 'cos you've got too much money and time!
Hey babe, what are you up to?
JAZZ
Just, err- hard at work in the studio.
NOT YET
That's looking good though. Will you exhibit it?
Yeah, thanks.

I mean, I say I don't mind these things, but I was already sulking when we got to the Chien Mort for Victor's self-organised surprise birthday party.

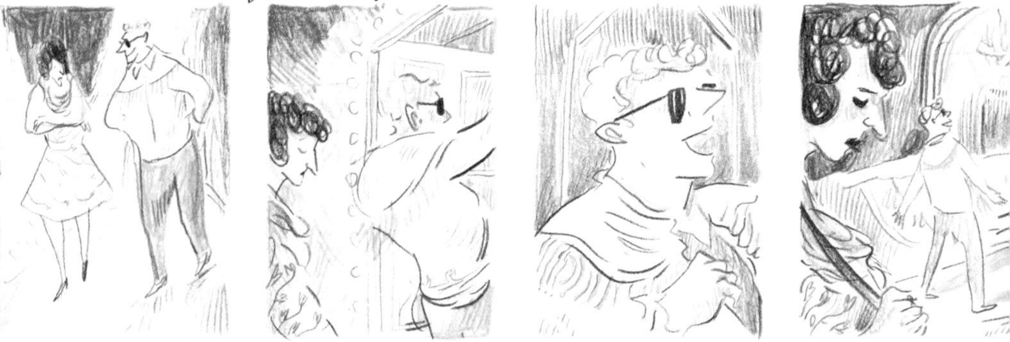

Half the gang were already there, and drunk. Victor's poet frien were huddled in the corner. Victor shouted "Don't worry guys, I' here!" as he came in, then he said it again as he got closer, to make sure everyone heard him. The gang erupted. Several people started clapping, as though Victor turning up to his own party wa either a surprise or an achievement.

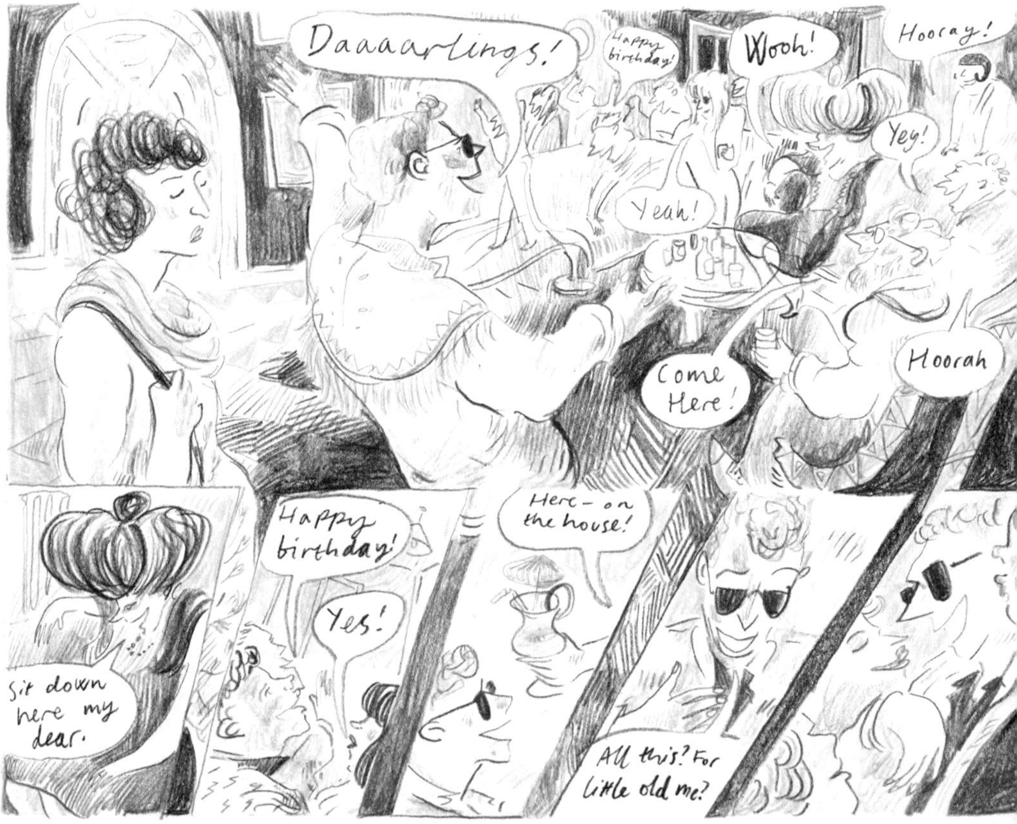
Daaaarlings!
Happy birthday!
Wooh!
Hooray!
Yey!
Yeah!
Come Here!
Hoorah
Sit down here my dear.
Happy birthday!
Yes!
Here – on the house!
All this? For little old me?

Penelope made an effort not to look at me. Or at least I suspect she did, though I made an effort not to look at her.

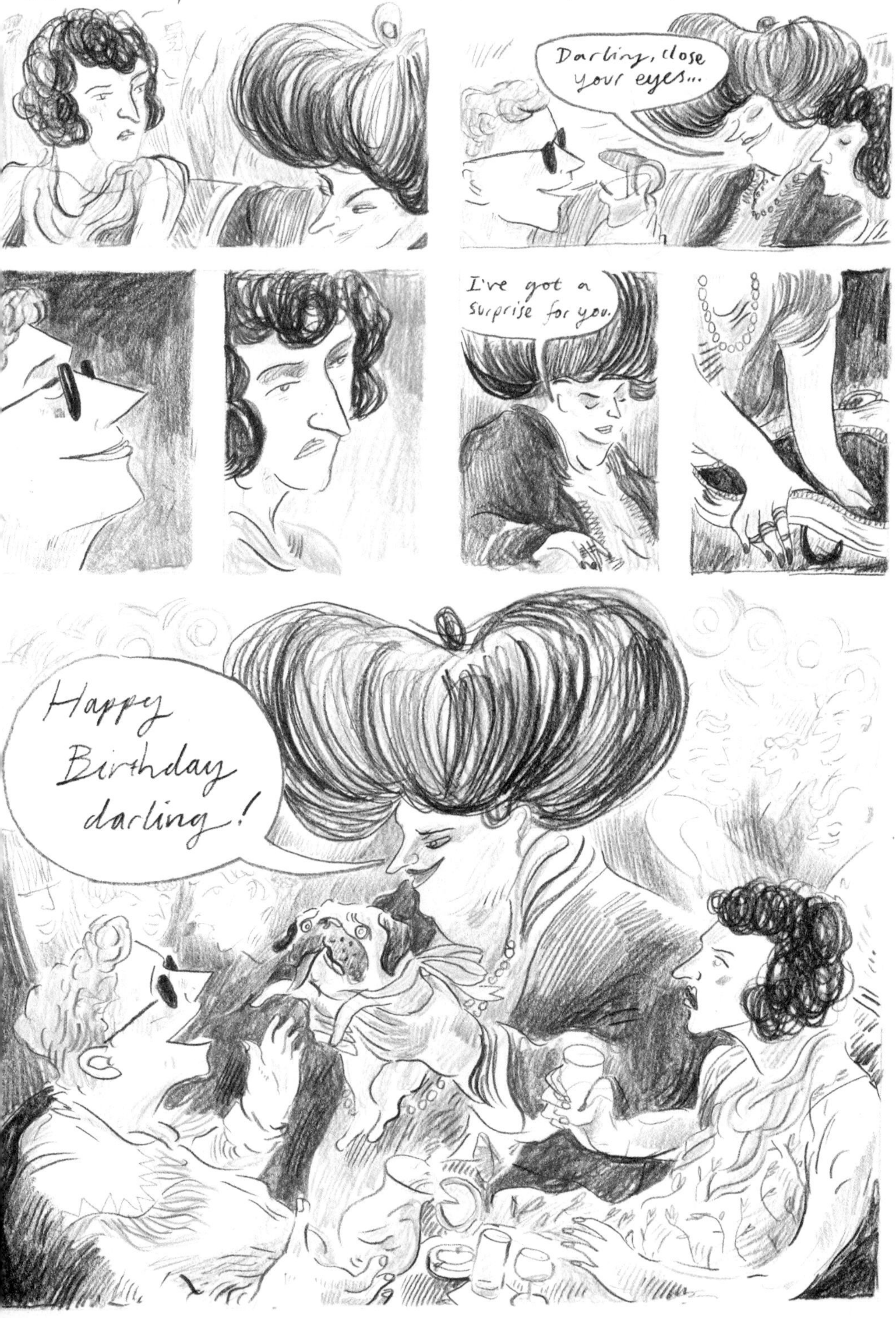
Darling, close your eyes...
I've got a surprise for you.
Happy Birthday darling!

Was it some sort of joke? Did she really want us to have a dog? We had never wanted a dog. Who would look after it? Did she really think Victor was capable of looking after a living, breathing dog? We had never wanted a dog.

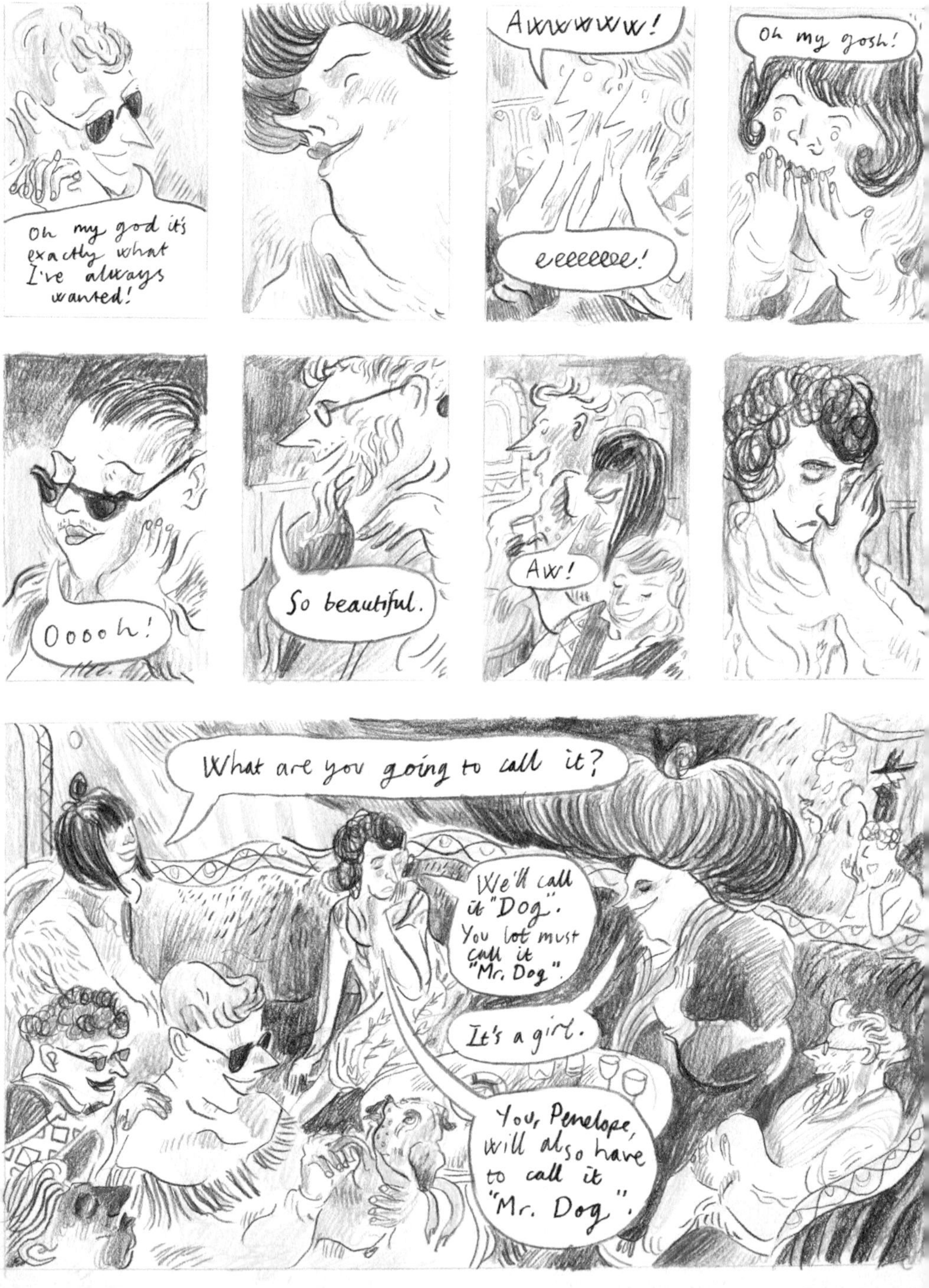

Oh my god it's exactly what I've always wanted!
Awwwwww!
eeeeeee!
Oh my gosh!
Ooooh!
So beautiful.
Aw!
What are you going to call it?
We'll call it "Dog". You lot must call it "Mr. Dog".
It's a girl.
You, Penelope, will also have to call it "Mr. Dog".

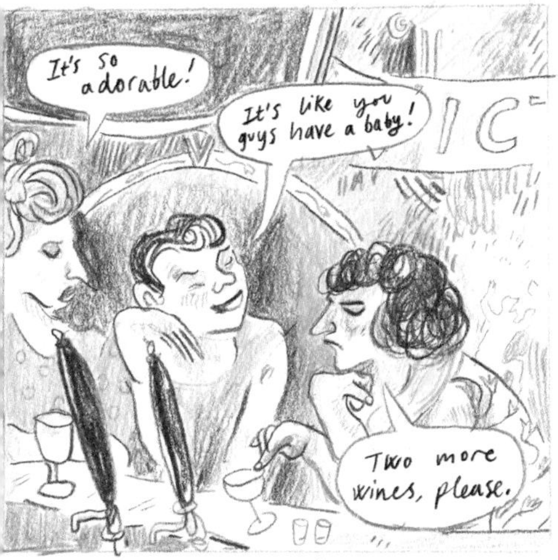
It's so adorable!
It's like you guys have a baby!
Two more wines, please.

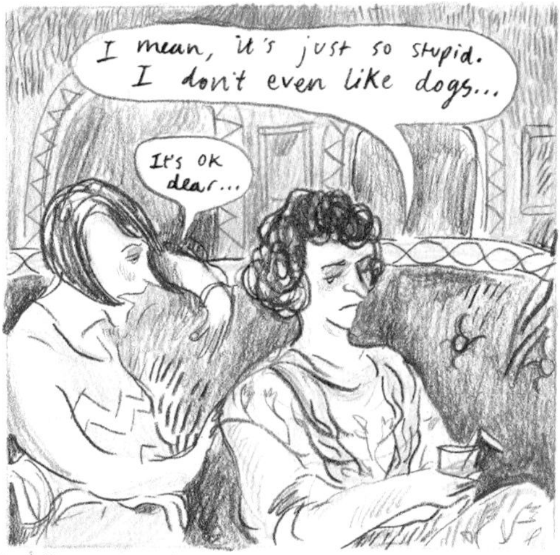
I mean, it's just so stupid. I don't even like dogs...
It's OK dear...

In the end, Victor decided to call it "Princess".

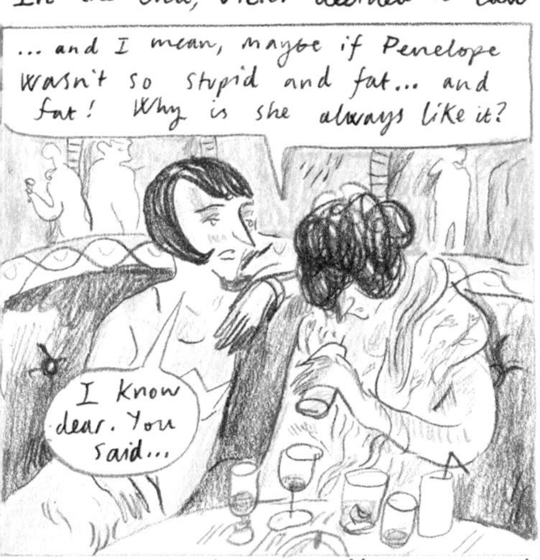
... and I mean, maybe if Penelope wasn't so stupid and fat... and fat! Why is she always like it?
I know dear. You said...

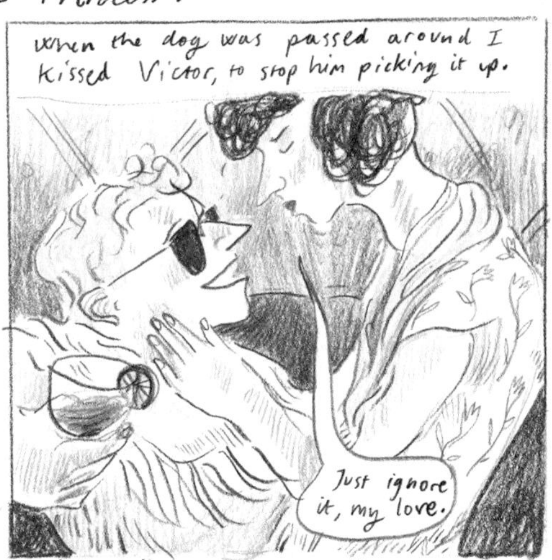
When the dog was passed around I kissed Victor, to stop him picking it up.
Just ignore it, my love.

In the end we couldn't go out dancing–"What if she gets lonely?" said Victor.
We had to walk home too, because it turns out you can't take dogs in taxis.

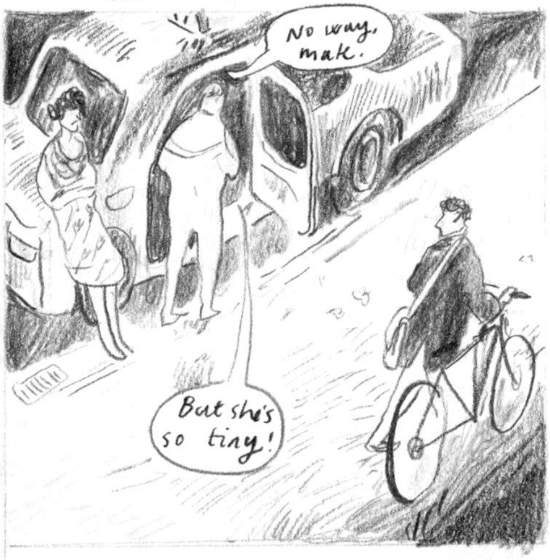
No way, mate.
But she's so tiny!

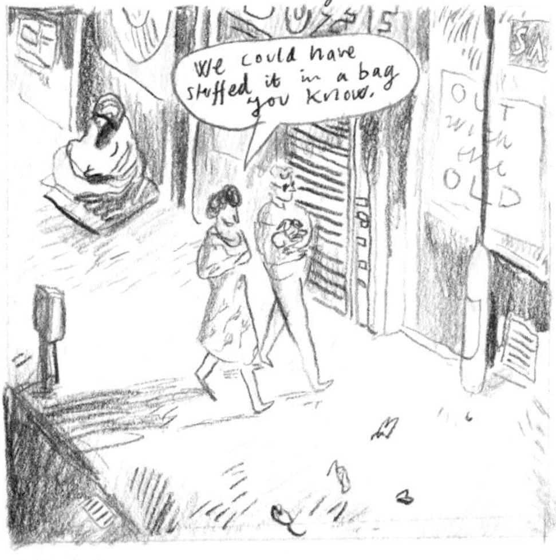
We could have stuffed it in a bag you know.

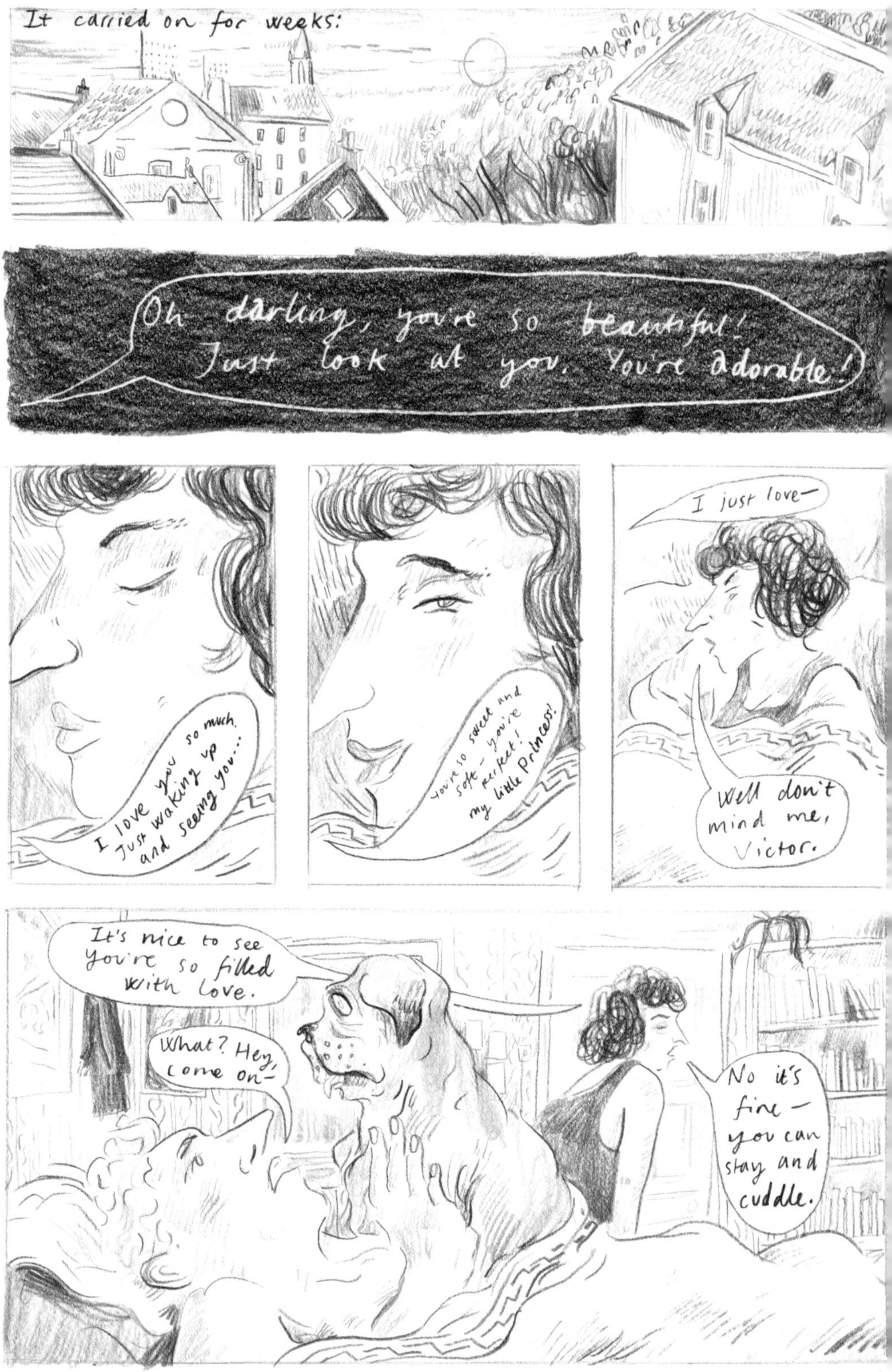
It carried on for weeks:
Oh darling, you're so beautiful! Just look at you. You're adorable!
I love you so much. Just waking up and seeing you...
You're so sweet and soft – you're perfect! my little Princess!
I just love–
Well don't mind me, Victor.
It's nice to see you're so filled with love.
What? Hey, come on–
No it's fine – you can stay and cuddle.

Victor's obsession with the dog only intensified. It meant an end to his poetry, which was a good thing, except the poetry never wet itself on the floor or sat up barking at foxes in the forest.

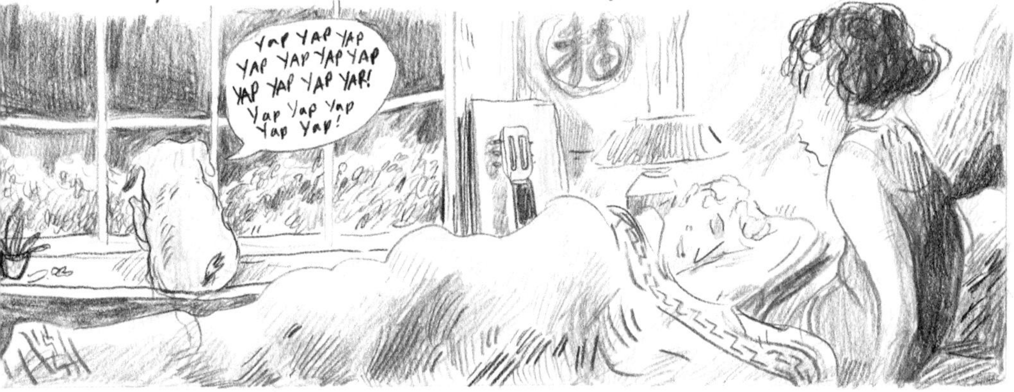
YAP YAP YAP
YAP YAP YAP YAP
YAP YAP YAP YAP!
Yap Yap Yap
Yap Yap!

I would come home to find him curled up with it, or feeding it, or trying on outfits with it. It chewed holes in his favourite boots, and he didn't mind. It chewed up several of my books too, and he still didn't mind.

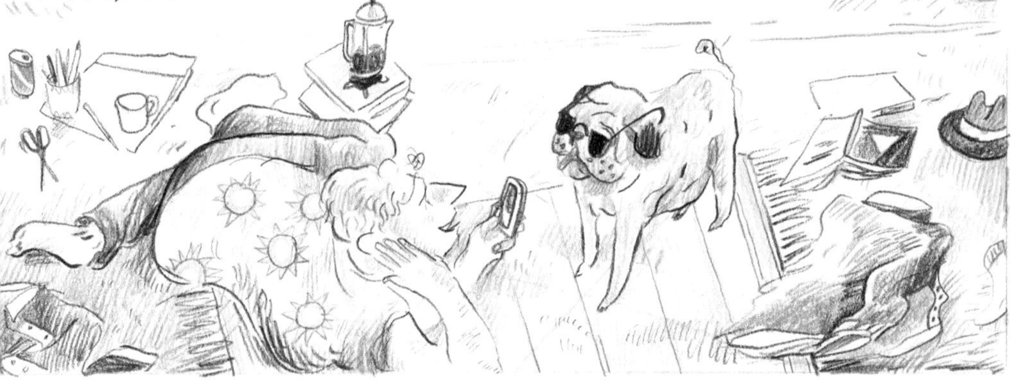

It even sat on his lap and ate meals off his plate.

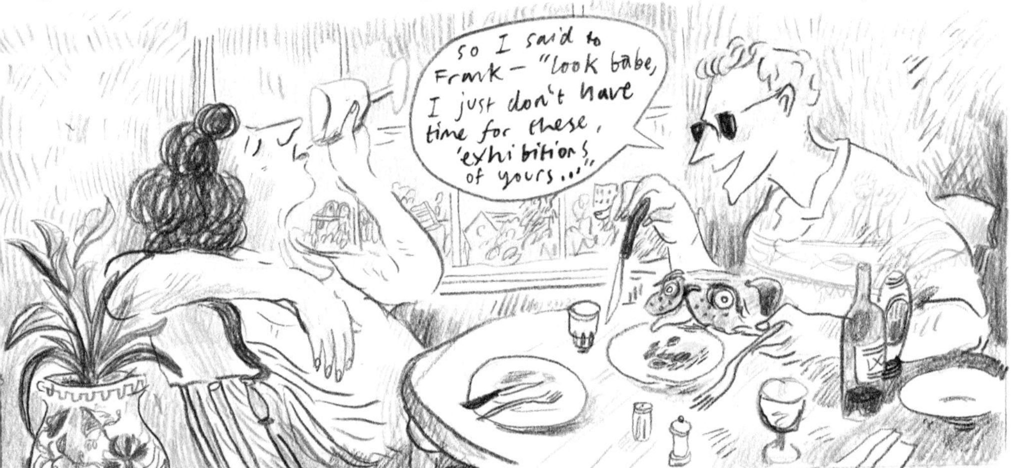
so I said to Frank— "look babe, I just don't have time for these, 'exhibitions' of yours..."

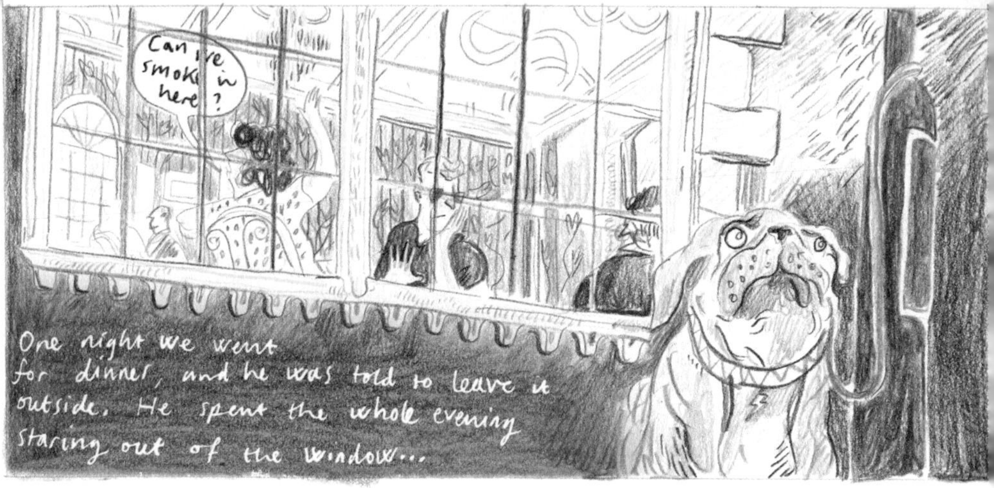
Can we smoke in here?
One night we went for dinner, and he was told to leave it outside. He spent the whole evening staring out of the window...

He would take it to nightclubs and sit at the side, no longer dancing, but surrounded by a new crowd of idiot sycophants.

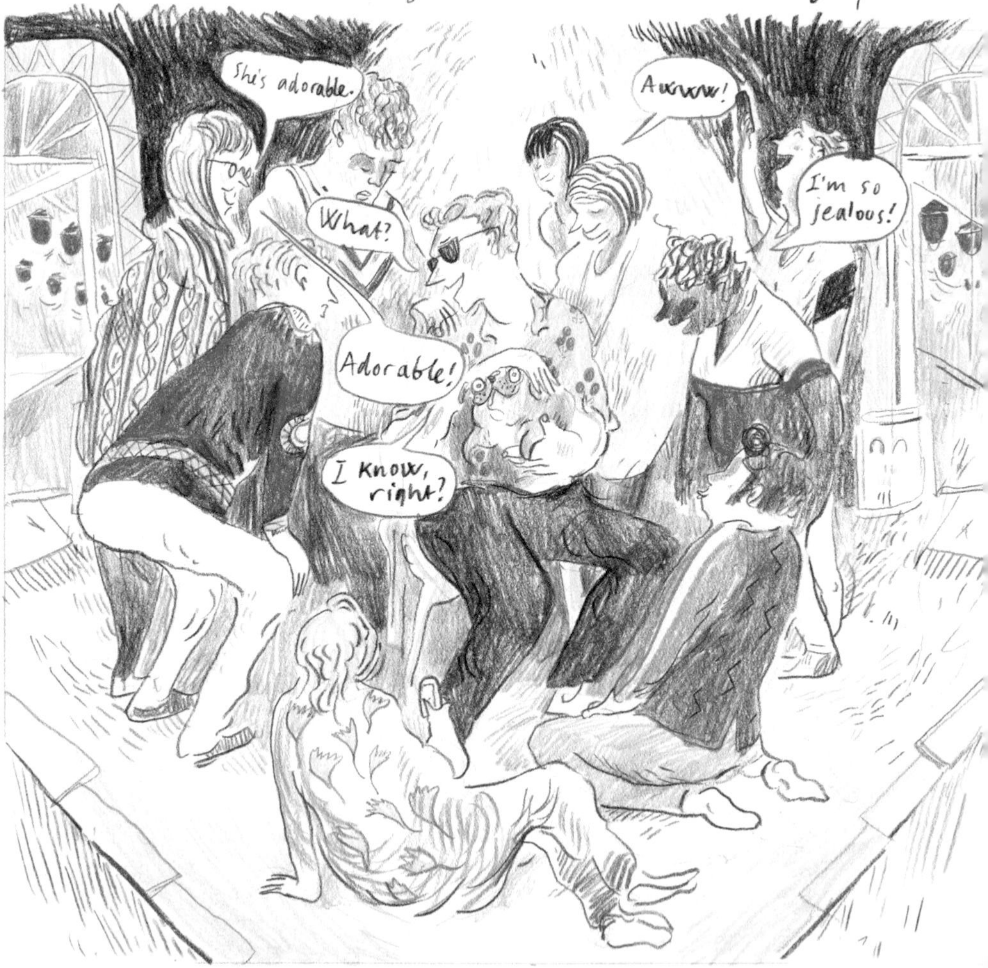
She's adorable.
Awwww!
What?
I'm so jealous!
Adorable!
I know, right?

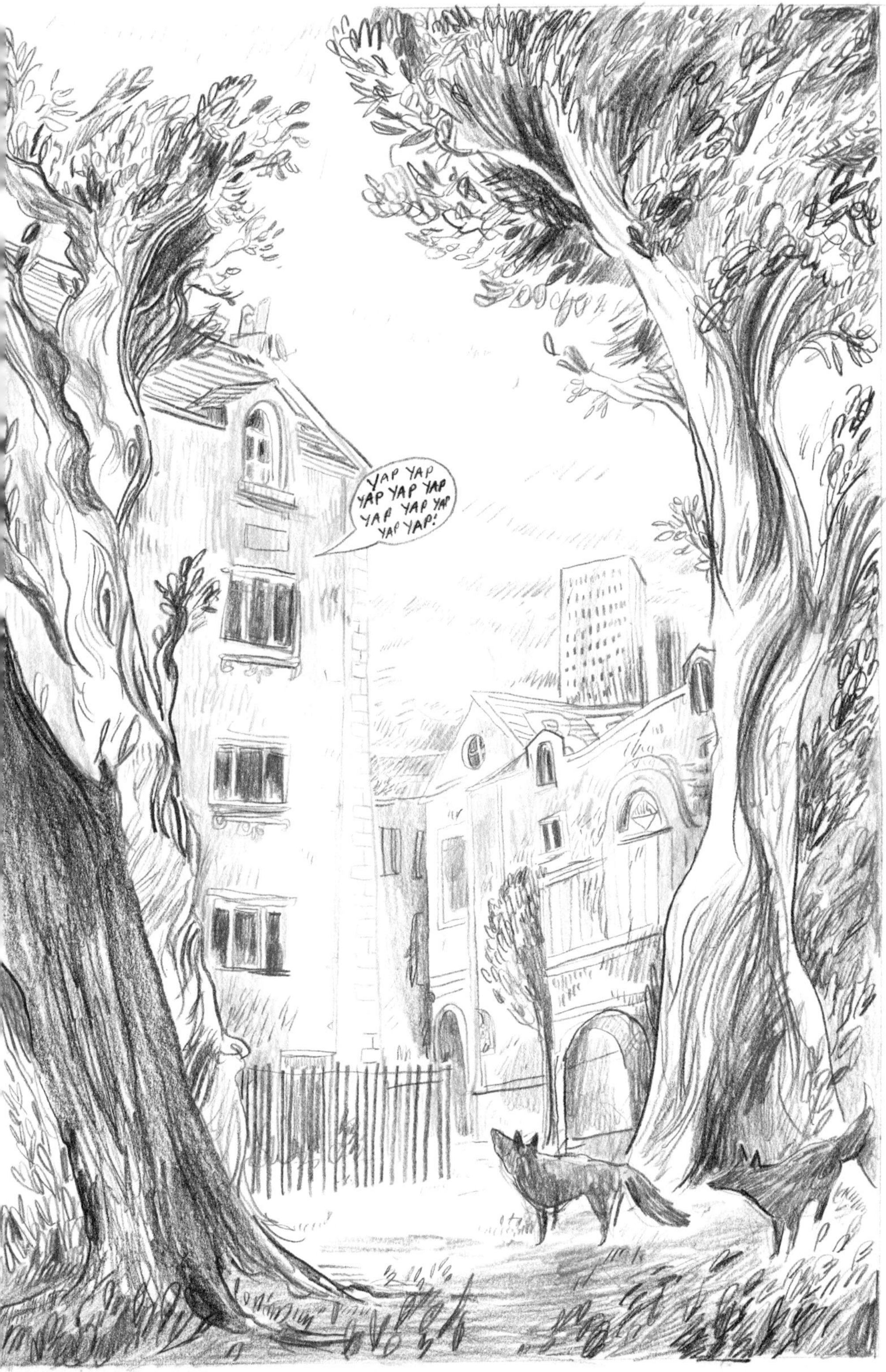
YAP YAP YAP YAP YAP YAP YAP YAP YAP YAP!

The dog wheezed rather than breathed, and smelt of sweat, old meat, and a sickening layer of Penelope's perfume.

I was in the bathroom of the Chien Mort, trying to scrub the smell off, when I was confronted with a strange vision.

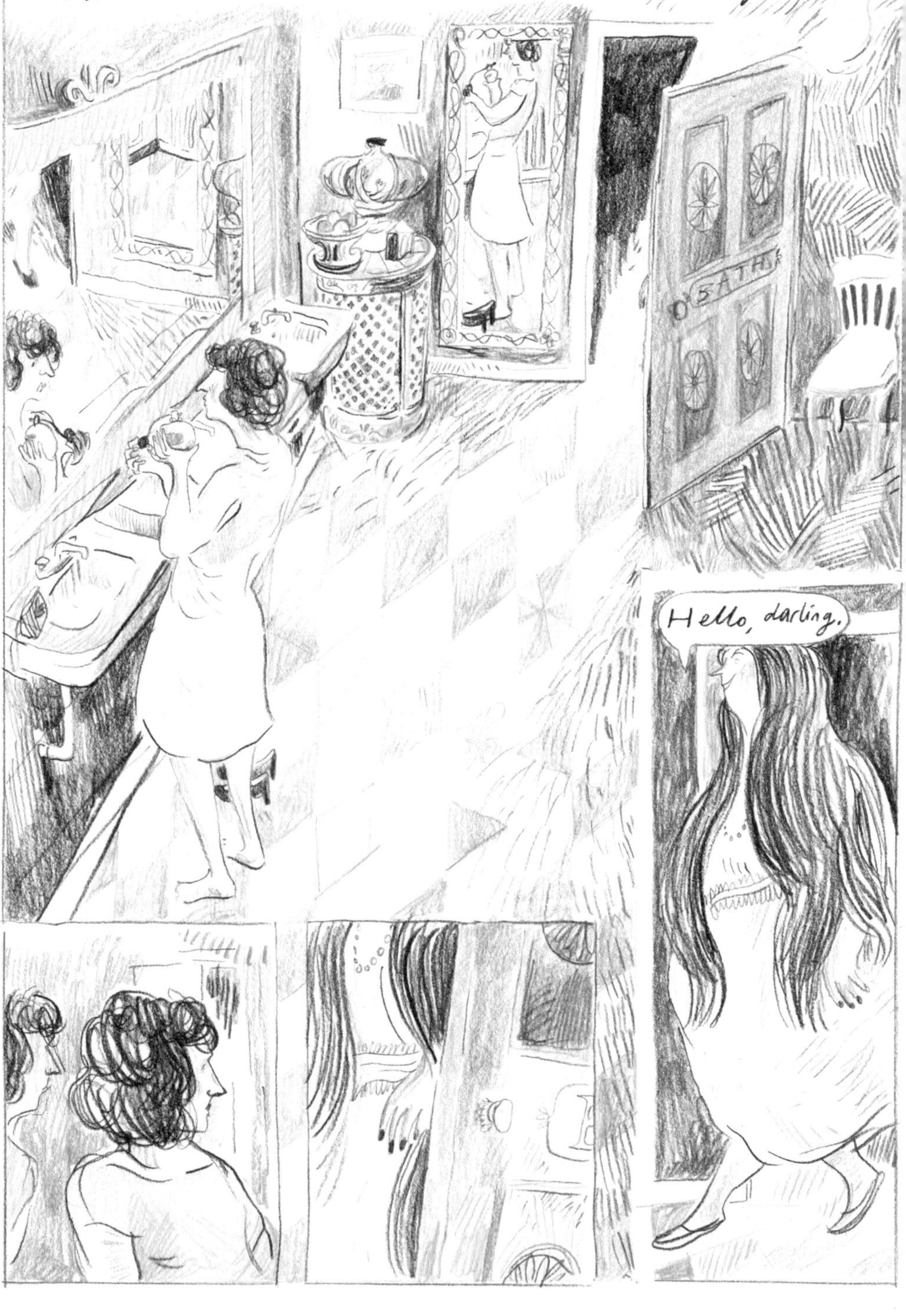
BATH
Hello, darling.

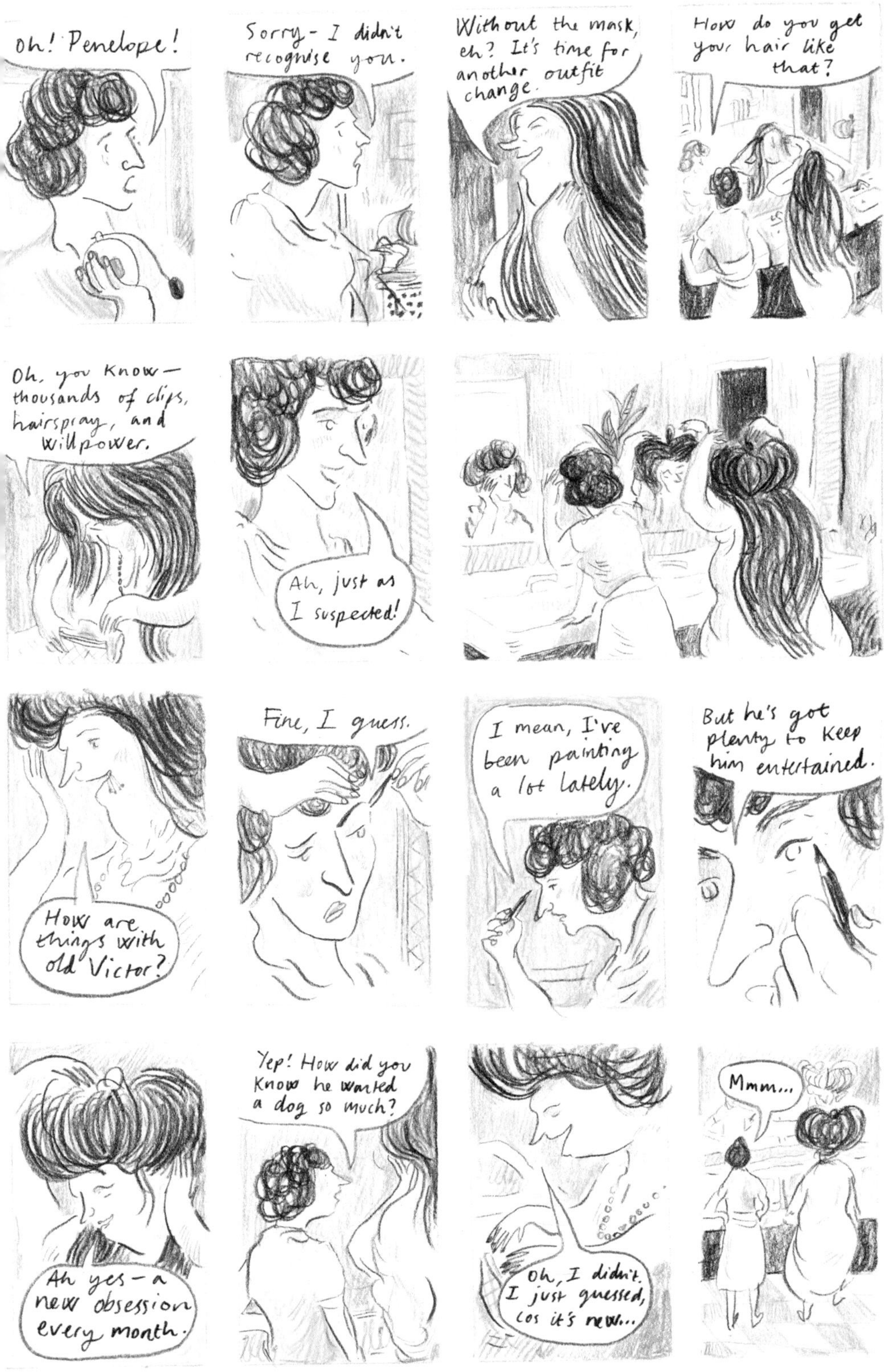
Oh! Penelope!
Sorry - I didn't recognise you.
Without the mask, eh? It's time for another outfit change.
How do you get your hair like that?
Oh, you know— thousands of clips, hairspray, and willpower.
Ah, just as I suspected!
How are things with old Victor?
Fine, I guess.
I mean, I've been painting a lot lately.
But he's got plenty to keep him entertained.
Ah yes—a new obsession every month.
Yep! How did you know he wanted a dog so much?
Oh, I didn't. I just guessed, cos it's new...
Mmm...

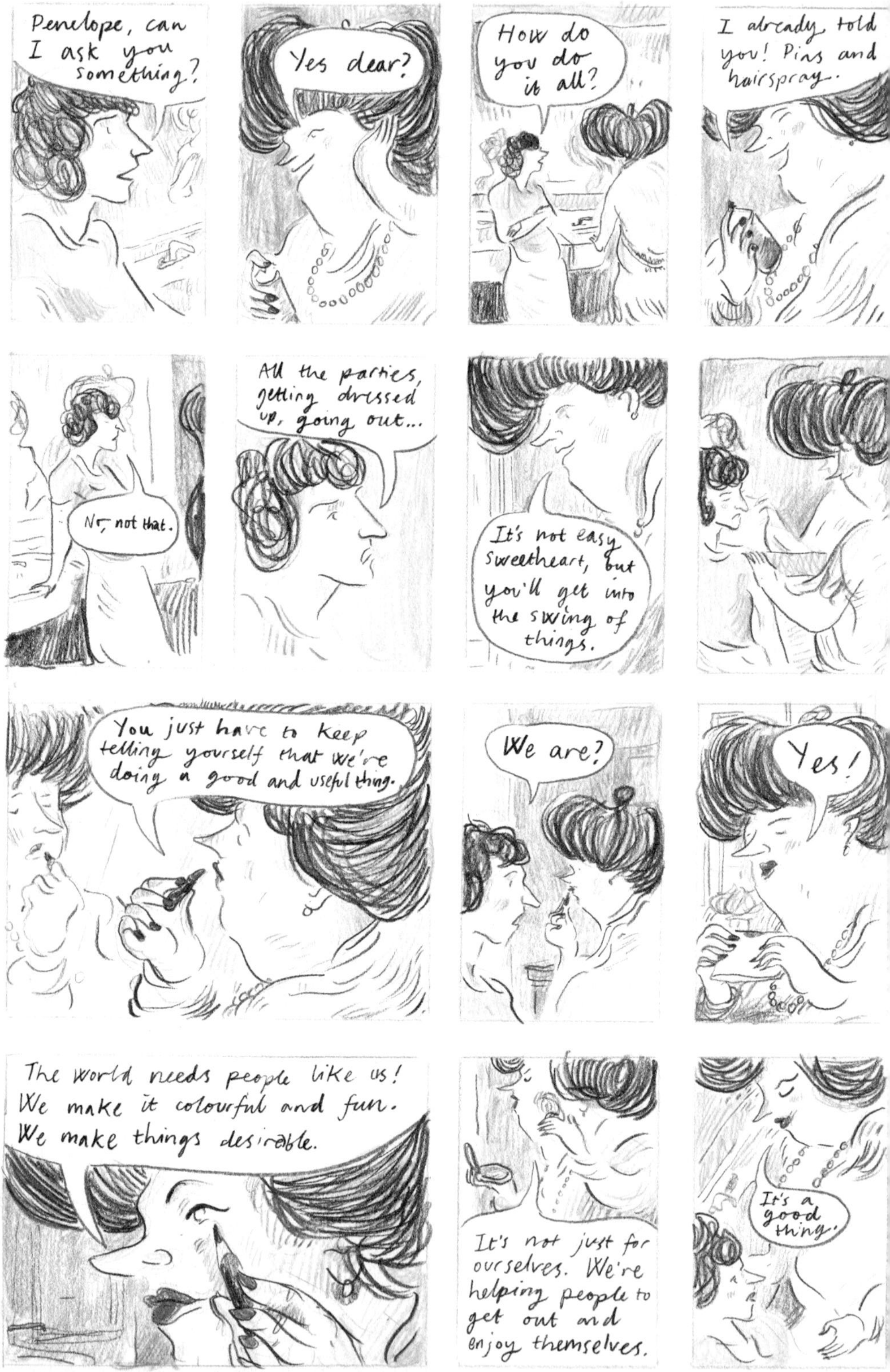
Penelope, can I ask you something?
Yes dear?
How do you do it all?
I already told you! Pins and hairspray.
No, not that.
All the parties, getting dressed up, going out...
It's not easy sweetheart, but you'll get into the swing of things.
You just have to keep telling yourself that we're doing a good and useful thing.
We are?
Yes!
The world needs people like us! We make it colourful and fun. We make things desirable.
It's not just for ourselves. We're helping people to get out and enjoy themselves.
It's a good thing.

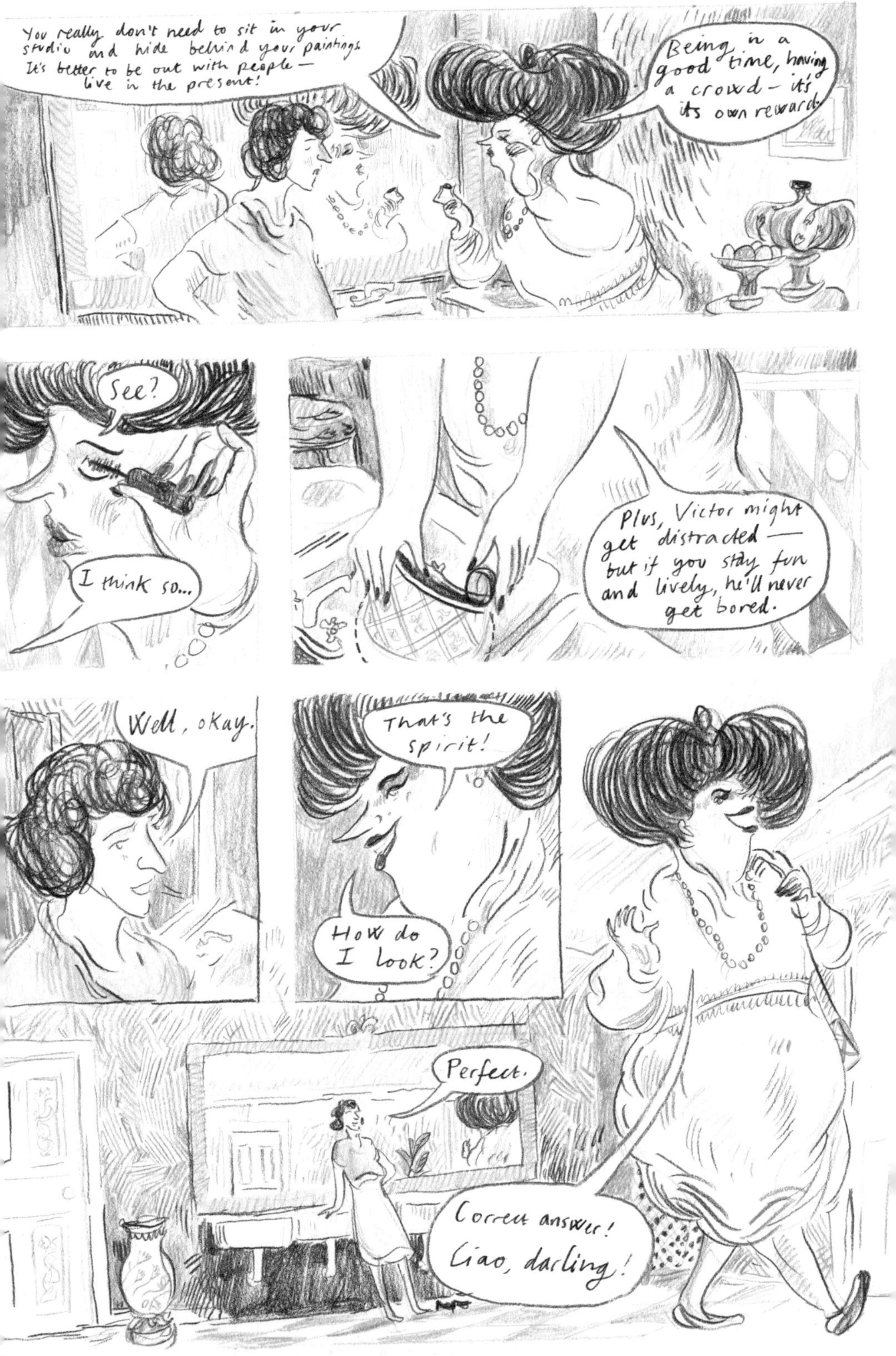

You really don't need to sit in your studio and hide behind your paintings. It's better to be out with people — live in the present!
Being in a good time, having a crowd — it's its own reward.
See?
I think so...
Plus, Victor might get distracted — but if you stay fun and lively, he'll never get bored.
Well, okay.
That's the spirit!
How do I look?
Perfect.
Correct answer! Ciao, darling!

With Penelope's advice in mind, I did go out more. And it's true - I did feel good living the glamorous life, with a crowd around me. I felt good to be dressed up, to be admired - and it distracted at least a little from Victor and his horrible dog.

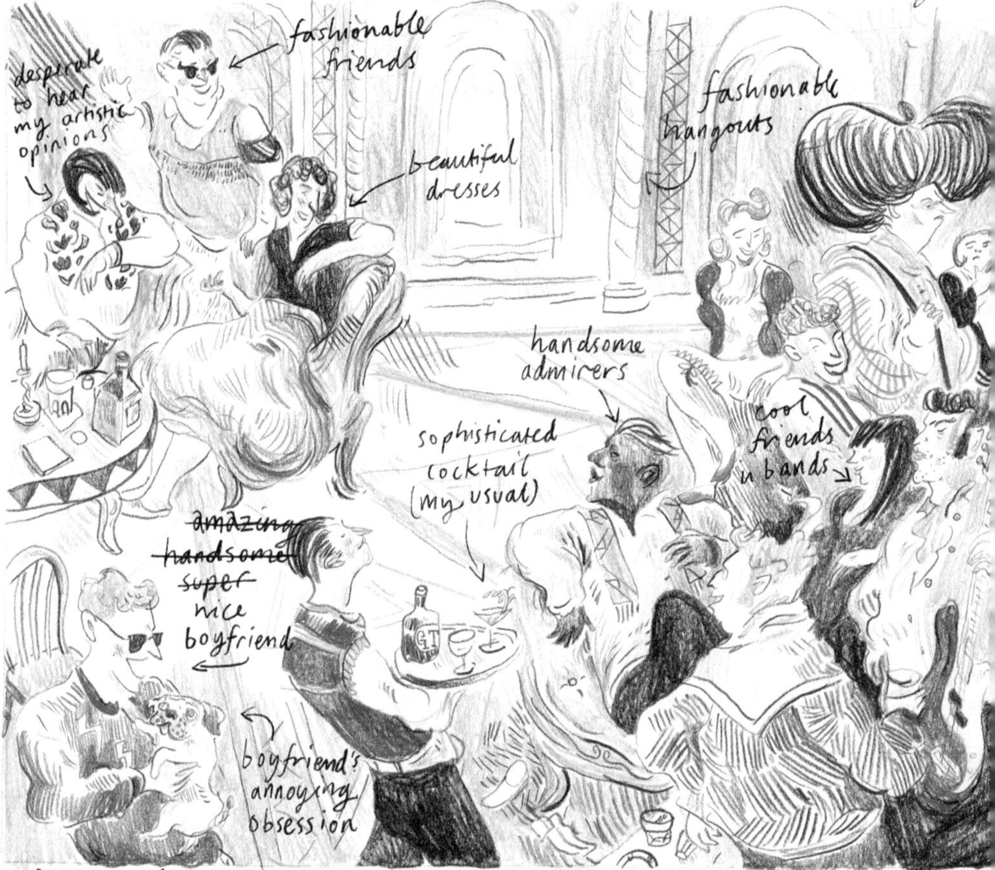
desperate to hear my artistic opinions
fashionable friends
beautiful dresses
fashionable hangouts
handsome admirers
cool friends n bands
sophisticated cocktail (my usual)
~~amazing~~ ~~handsome~~ ~~super~~ nice boyfriend
boyfriend's annoying obsession

On the other hand, it kept me away from painting a little too often.

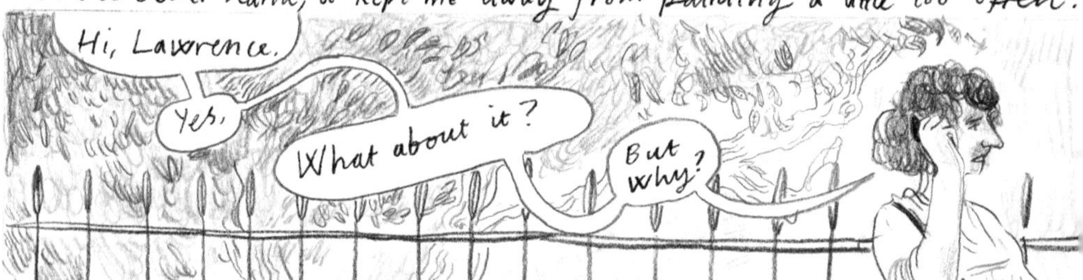
Hi, Lawrence.
Yes,
What about it?
But why?

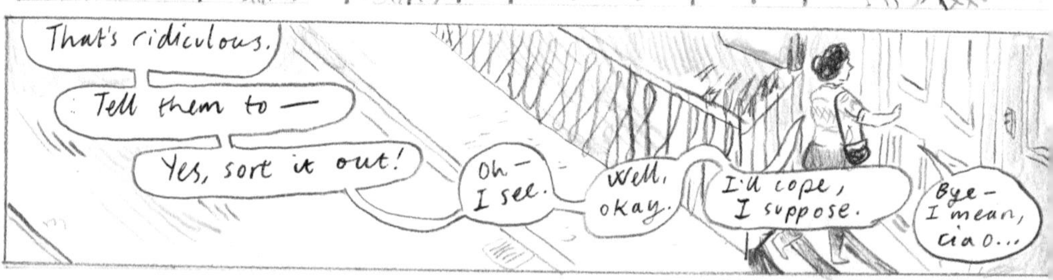
That's ridiculous.
Tell them to —
Yes, sort it out!
Oh - I see.
Well, okay.
I'll cope, I suppose.
Bye - I mean, ciao...

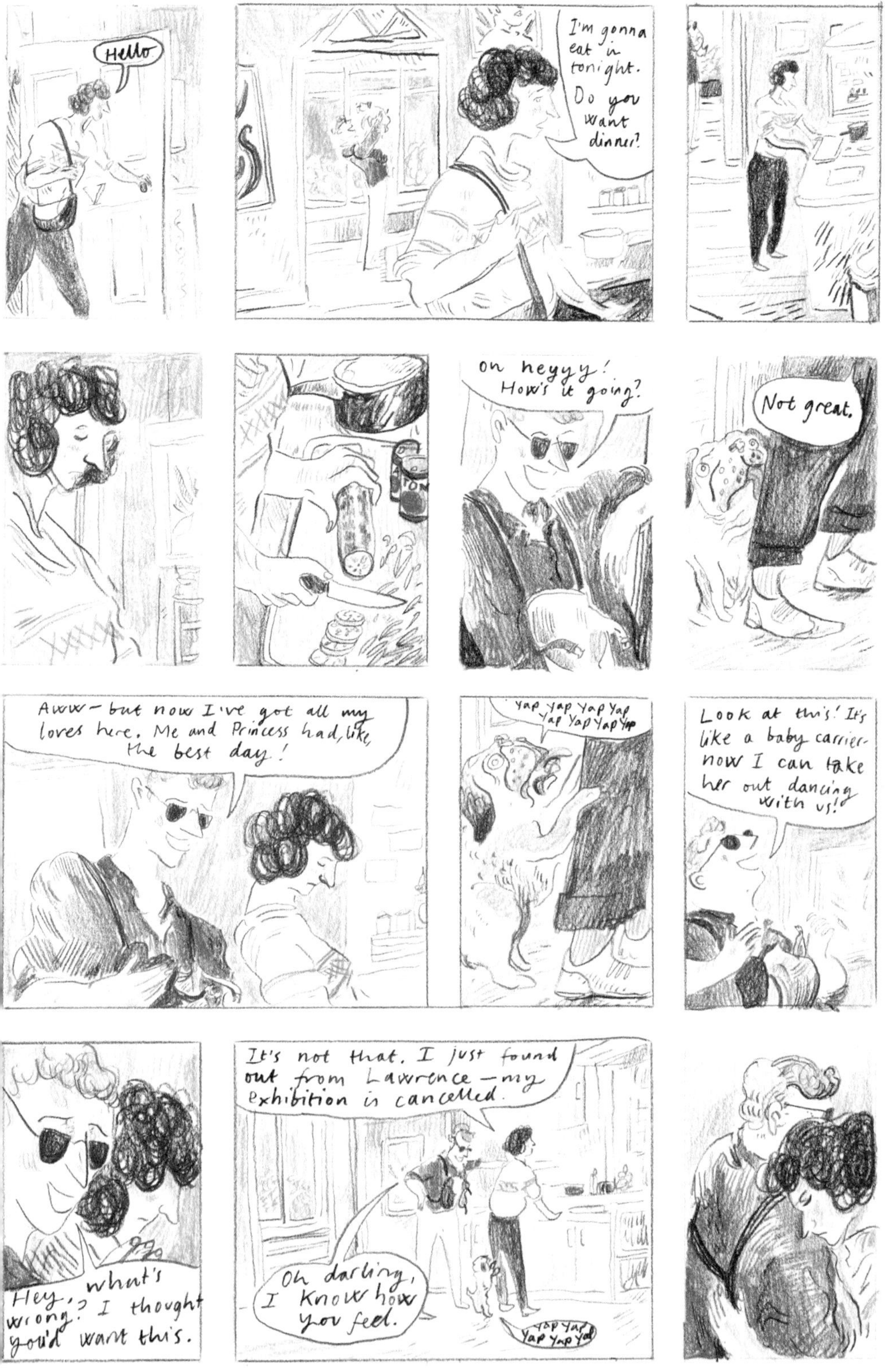
Hello
I'm gonna eat in tonight. Do you want dinner?
Oh heyyy! How's it going?
Not great.
Aww—but now I've got all my loves here. Me and Princess had, like, the best day!
Yap Yap Yap Yap Yap Yap Yap Yap
Look at this! It's like a baby carrier—now I can take her out dancing with us!
Hey, what's wrong? I thought you'd want this.
It's not that. I just found out from Lawrence—my exhibition is cancelled.
Oh darling, I know how you feel.
Yap Yap Yap Yap Yap

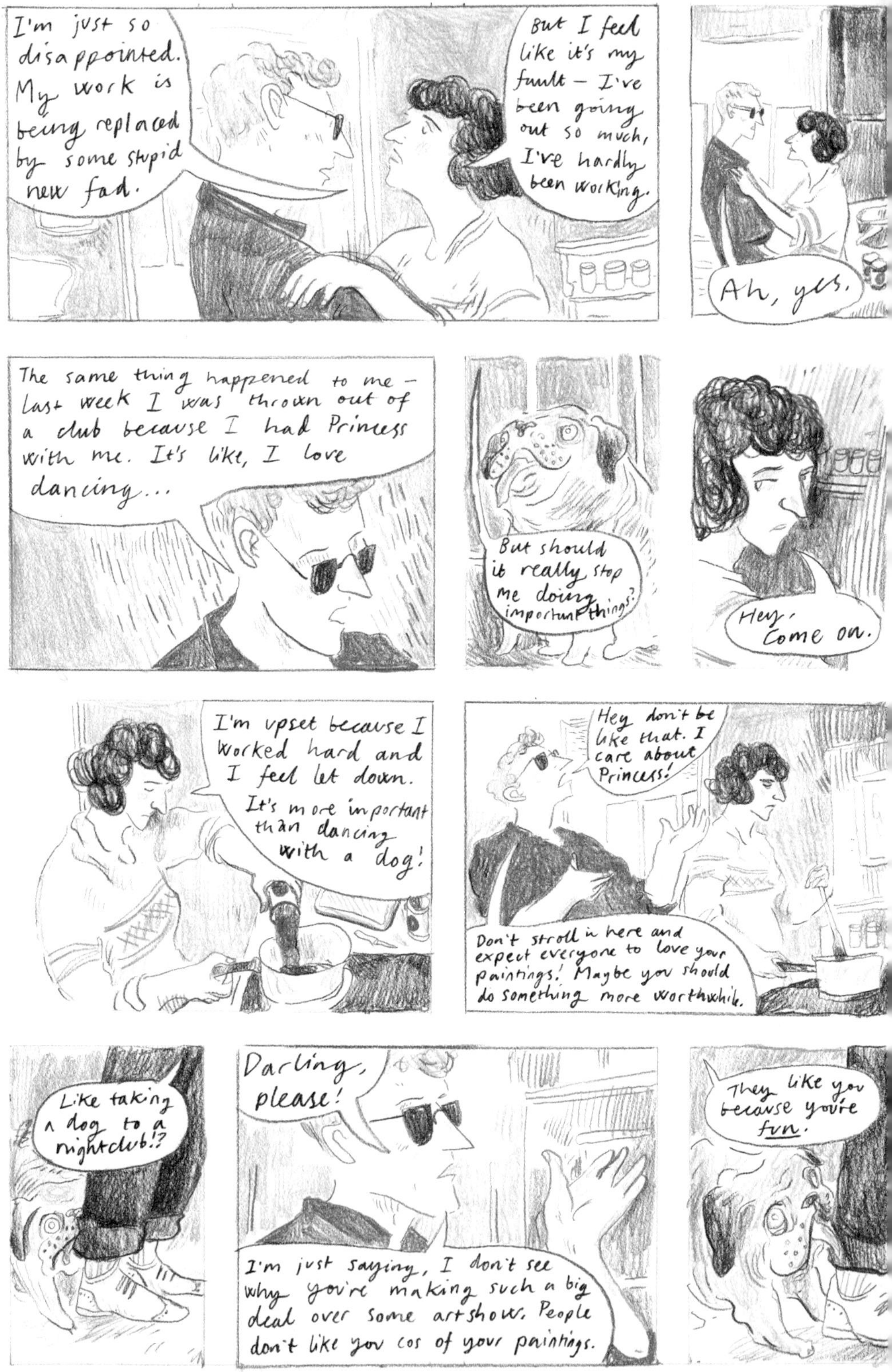
I'm just so disappointed. My work is being replaced by some stupid new fad.
But I feel like it's my fault – I've been going out so much, I've hardly been working.
Ah, yes.
The same thing happened to me – last week I was thrown out of a club because I had Princess with me. It's like, I love dancing...
But should it really stop me doing important things?
Hey. Come on.
I'm upset because I worked hard and I feel let down. It's more important than dancing with a dog!
Hey don't be like that. I care about Princess!
Don't stroll in here and expect everyone to love your paintings! Maybe you should do something more worthwhile.
Like taking a dog to a nightclub!?
Darling, please!
I'm just saying, I don't see why you're making such a big deal over some art show. People don't like you cos of your paintings.
They like you because you're fun.

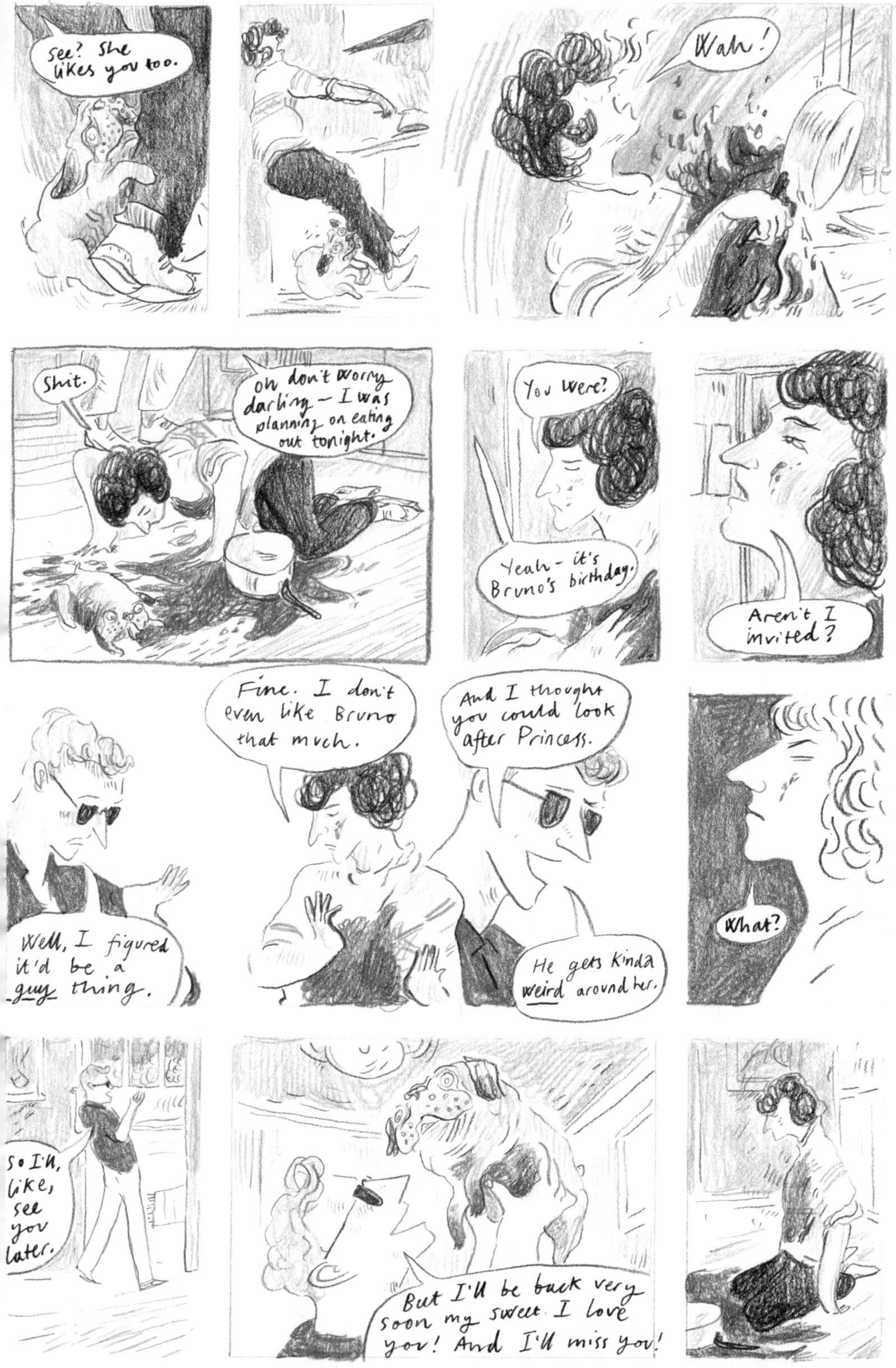
See? She likes you too.
Wah!
Shit.
Oh don't worry darling – I was planning on eating out tonight.
You were?
Yeah – it's Bruno's birthday.
Aren't I invited?
Well, I figured it'd be a guy thing.
Fine. I don't even like Bruno that much.
And I thought you could look after Princess.
He gets kinda weird around her.
What?
So I'll, like, see you later.
But I'll be back very soon my sweet. I love you! And I'll miss you!

So that's fine then. Fine. Obviously Victor can just stroll off with his friend whenever he wants. Fine. Even though I'm upset and he obviously doesn't even care at all, which is totally ridiculous because I actually work hard on these things and all he ever does is sit around with his lazy friends and his disgusting dog which I'm supposed to put up with, just like I'm supposed to put up with his stupid poetry, even when I'd quite like to see his friends too becau I actually quite like Bruno and being with just about any of them would be better than being with him and his stupid stupi stupid **Dog**

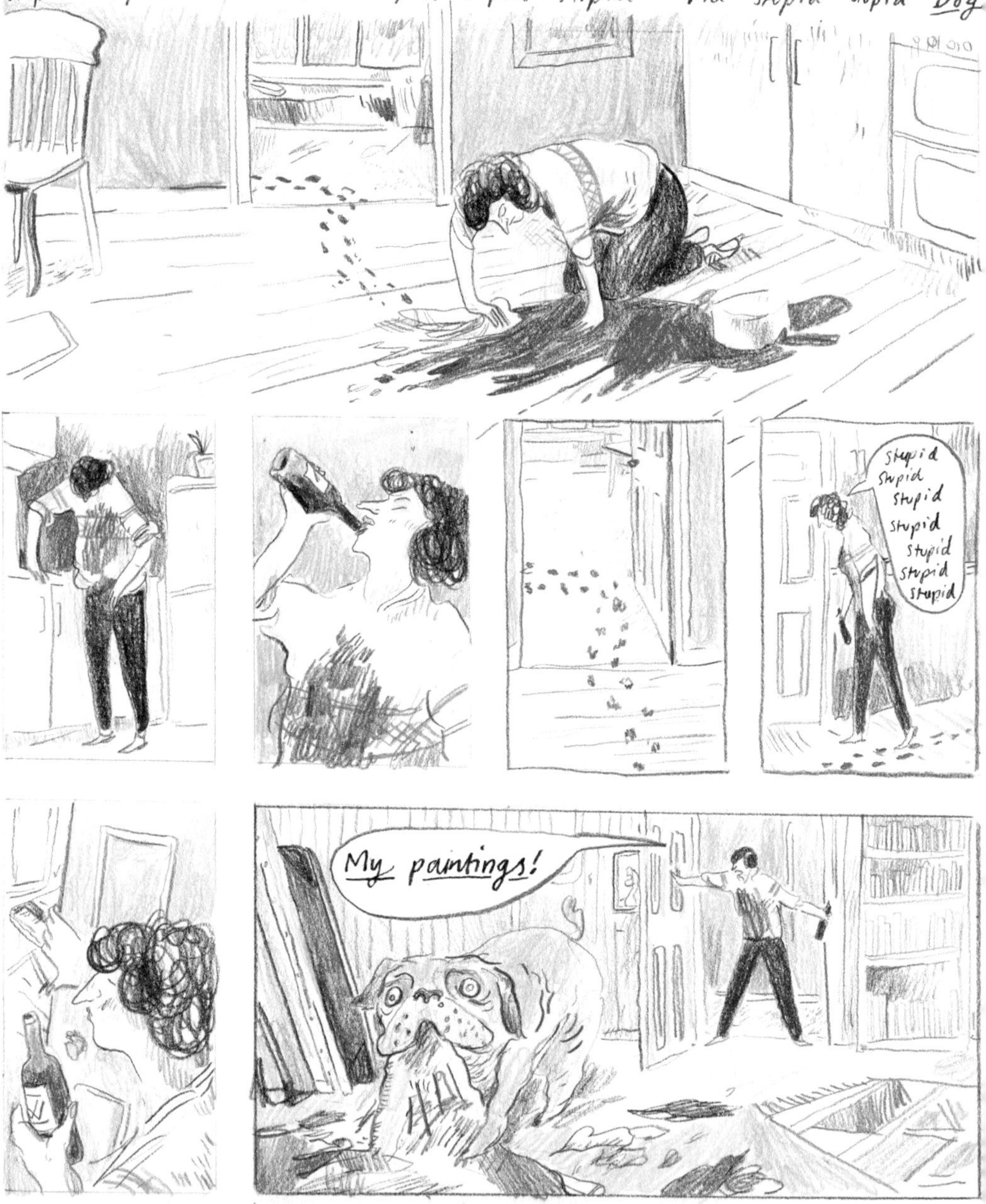
stupid stupid stupid stupid stupid stupid stupid
My paintings!

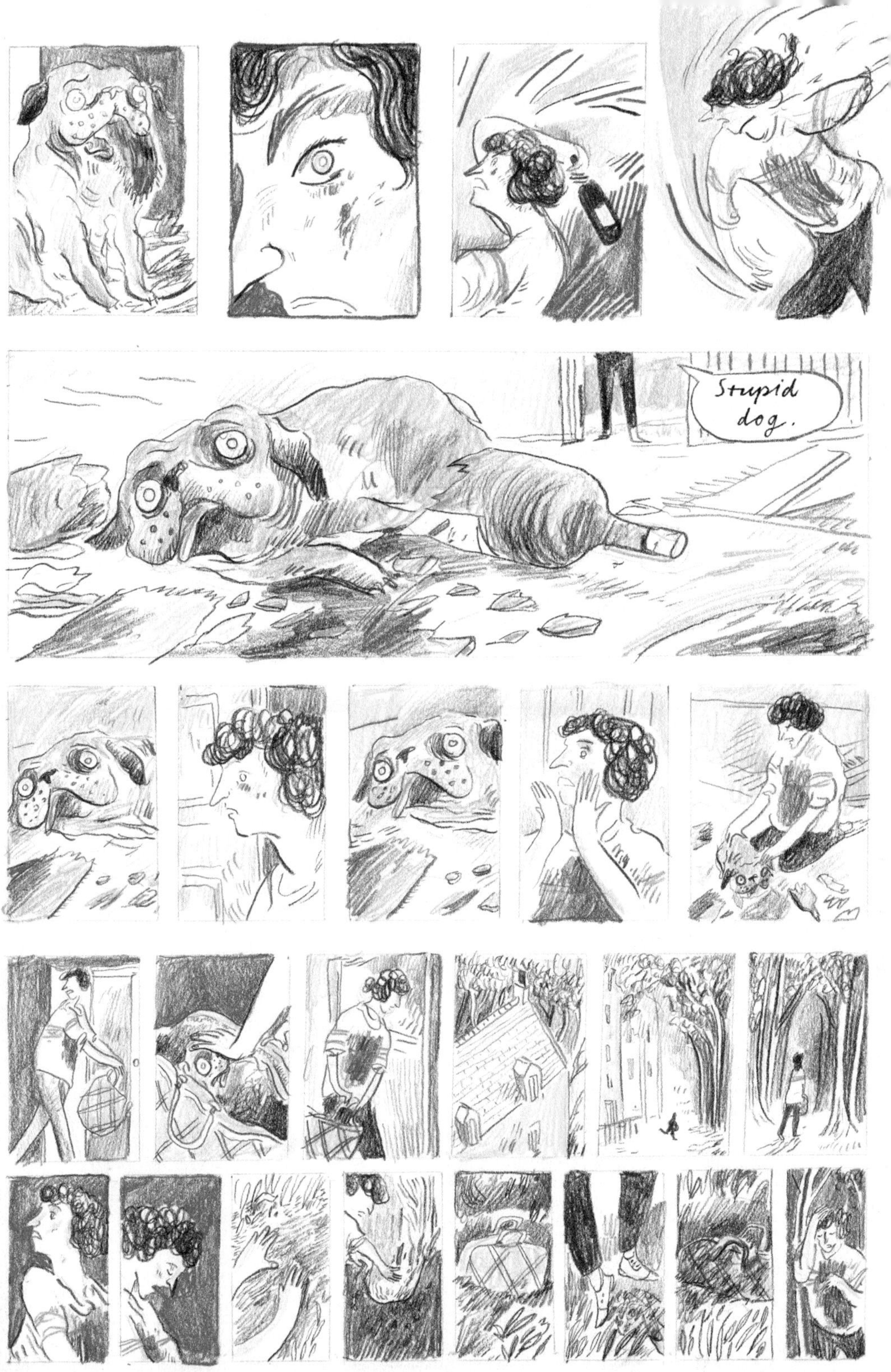
Stupid dog.

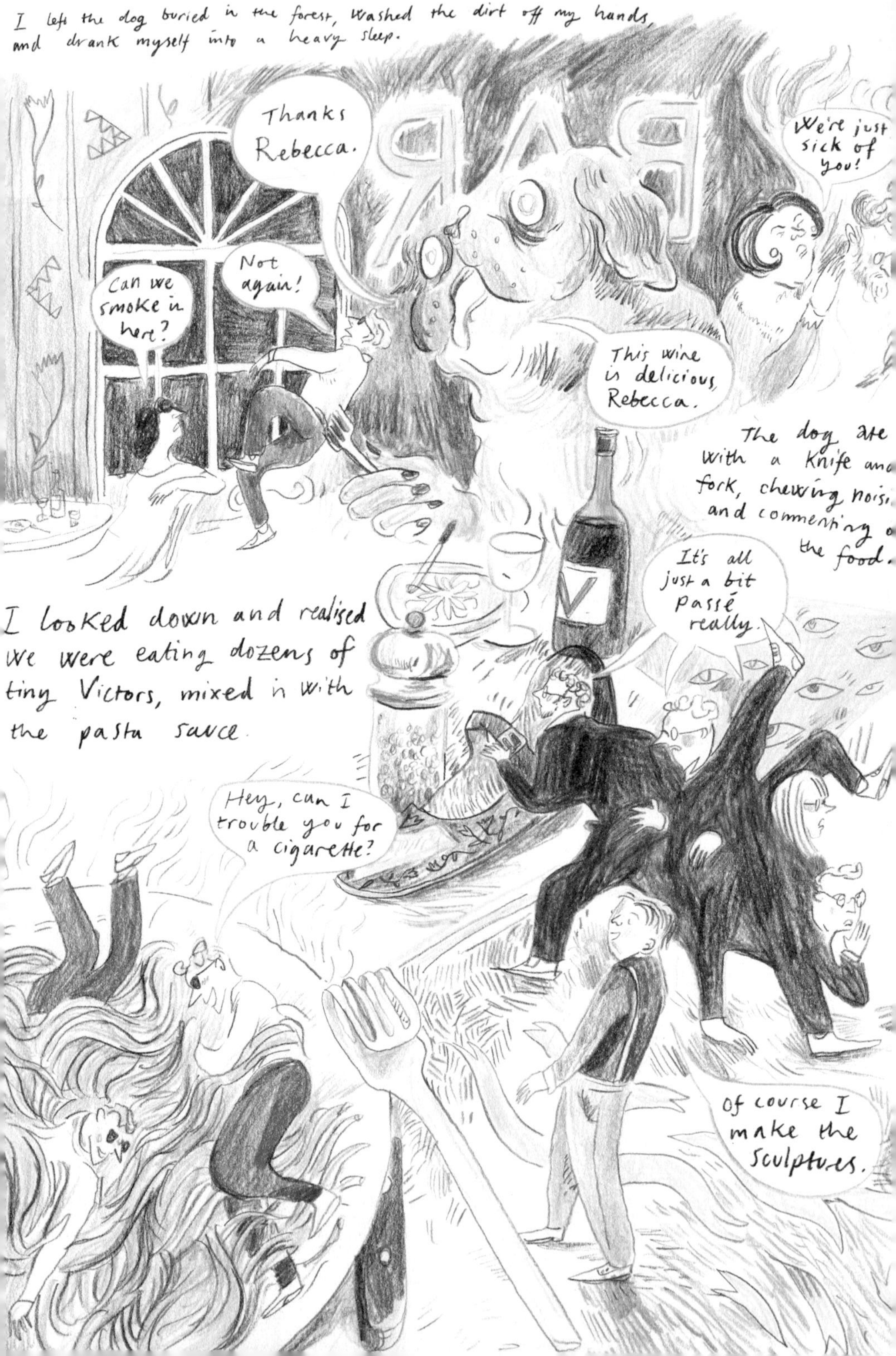
I left the dog buried in the forest, washed the dirt off my hands, and drank myself into a heavy sleep.
Thanks Rebecca.
Can we smoke in here?
Not again!
We're just sick of you!
This wine is delicious, Rebecca.
The dog ate with a knife an fork, chewing noisi and commenting o the food.
It's all just a bit passé really.
I looked down and realised we were eating dozens of tiny Victors, mixed in with the pasta sauce.
Hey, can I trouble you for a cigarette?
Of course I make the sculptures.

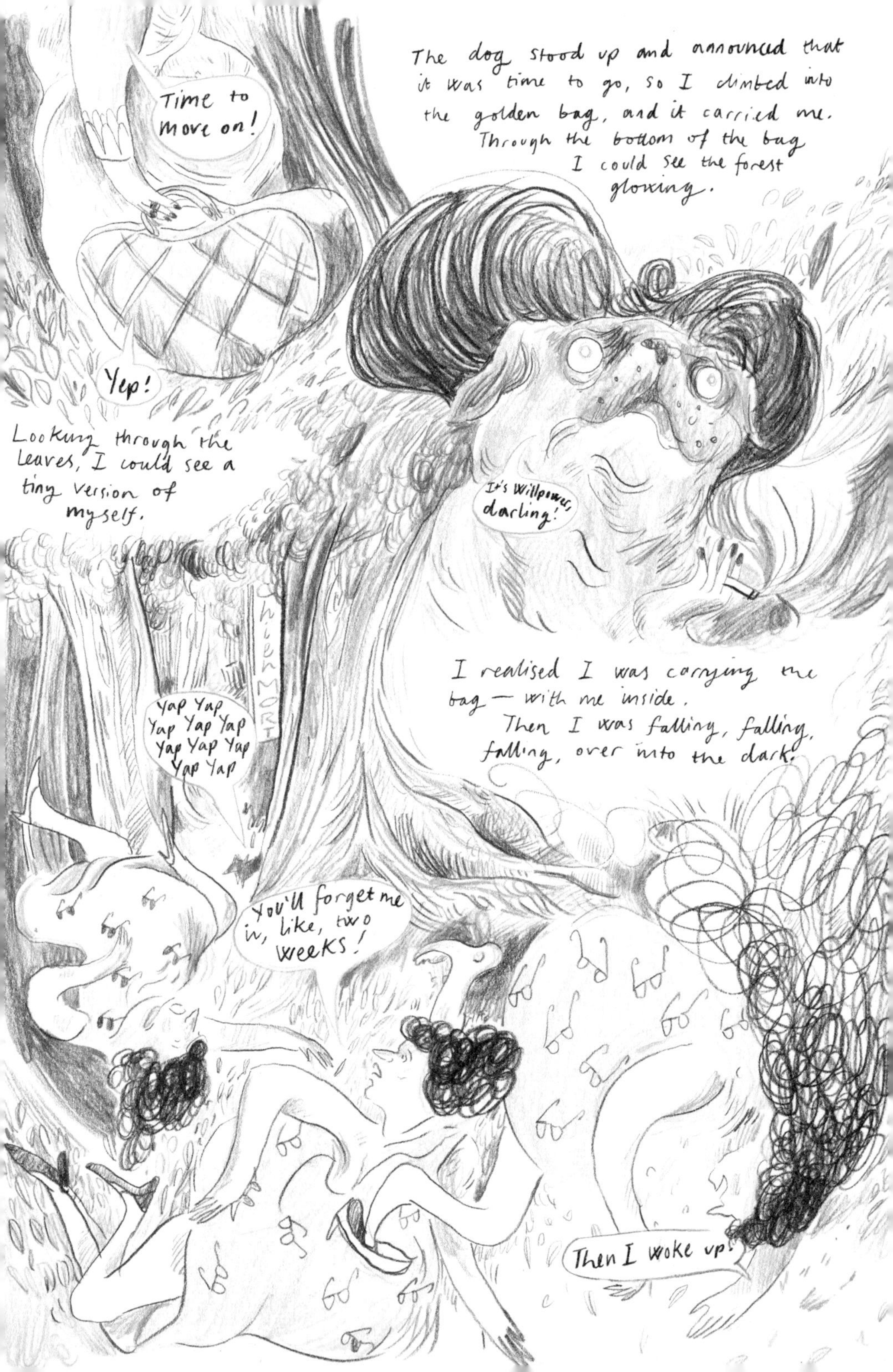

Time to move on!
The dog stood up and announced that it was time to go, so I climbed into the golden bag, and it carried me. Through the bottom of the bag I could see the forest glowing.
Yep!
Looking through the leaves, I could see a tiny version of myself.
It's Willpower, darling!
I realised I was carrying the bag — with me inside. Then I was falling, falling, falling, over into the dark.
Yap Yap Yap Yap Yap Yap Yap Yap Yap Yap
You'll forget me in, like, two weeks!
Then I woke up!

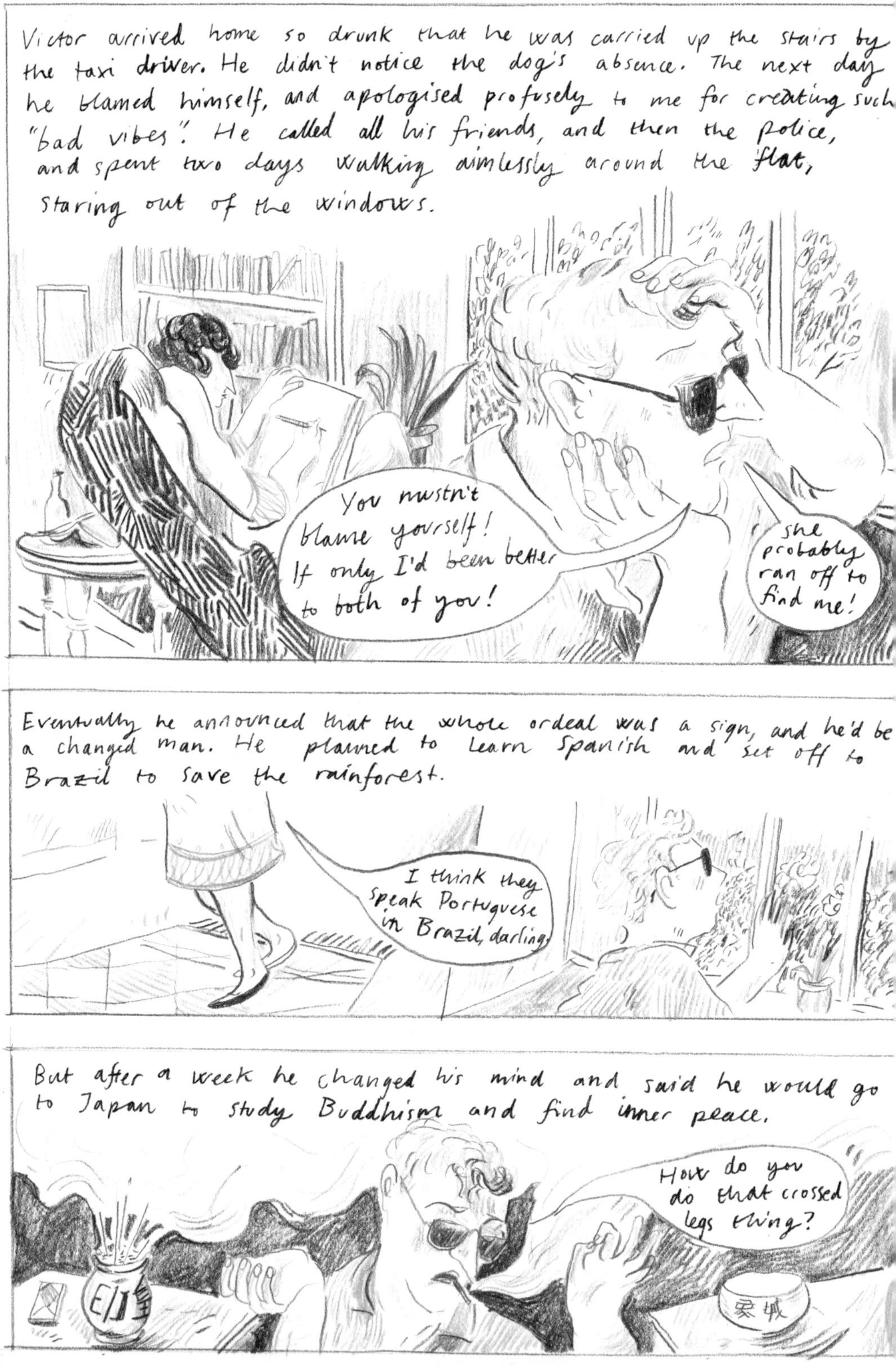
Victor arrived home so drunk that he was carried up the stairs by the taxi driver. He didn't notice the dog's absence. The next day he blamed himself, and apologised profusely to me for creating such "bad vibes". He called all his friends, and then the police, and spent two days walking aimlessly around the flat, staring out of the windows.
You mustn't blame yourself! If only I'd been better to both of you!
She probably ran off to find me!
Eventually he announced that the whole ordeal was a sign, and he'd be a changed man. He planned to learn Spanish and set off to Brazil to save the rainforest.
I think they speak Portuguese in Brazil, darling.
But after a week he changed his mind and said he would go to Japan to study Buddhism and find inner peace.
How do you do that crossed legs thing?

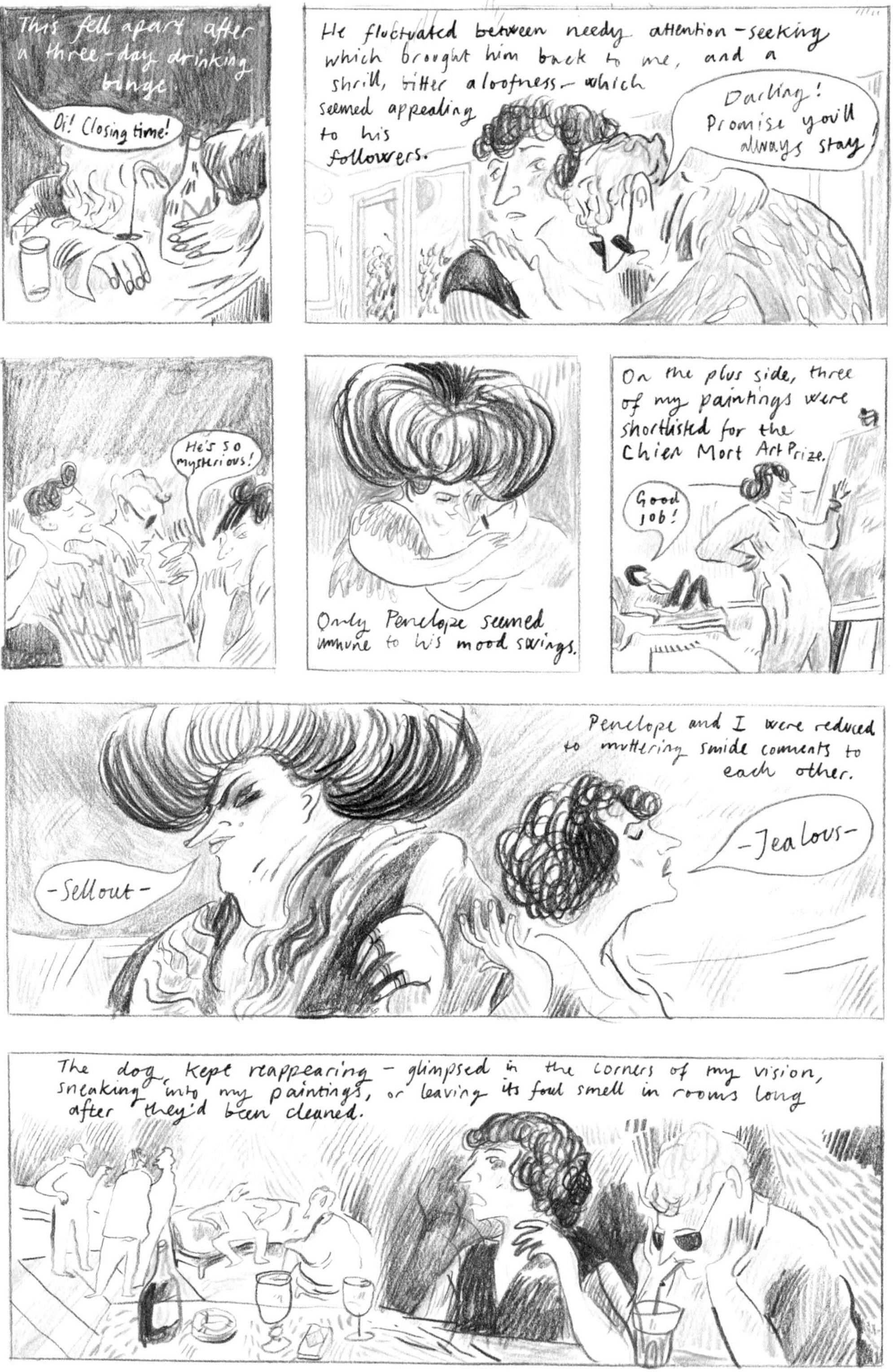
This fell apart after a three-day drinking binge.
Oi! Closing time!
He fluctuated between needy attention-seeking which brought him back to me, and a shrill, bitter aloofness - which seemed appealing to his followers.
Darling! Promise you'll always stay!
He's so mysterious!
Only Penelope seemed immune to his mood swings.
On the plus side, three of my paintings were shortlisted for the Chien Mort Art Prize.
Good job!
Penelope and I were reduced to muttering snide comments to each other.
-Sellout-
-Jealous-
The dog kept reappearing - glimpsed in the corners of my vision, sneaking into my paintings, or leaving its foul smell in rooms long after they'd been cleaned.

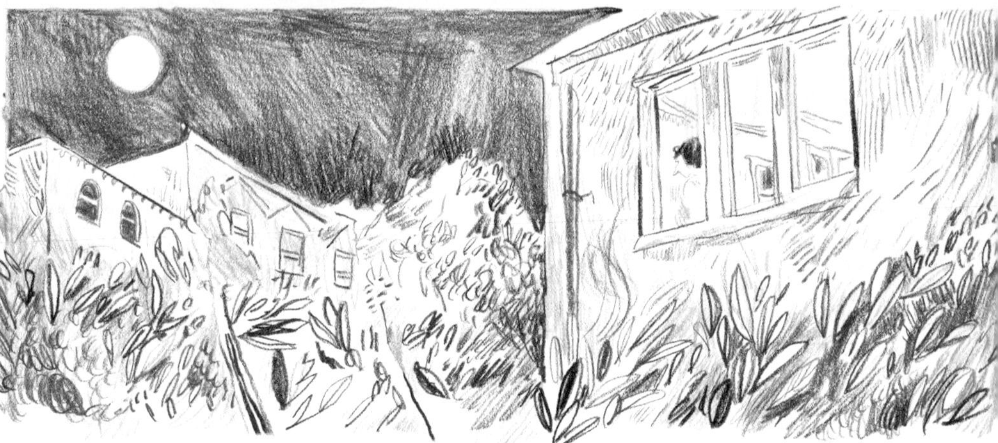

The passing weeks brought on an aura of madness, mania and desperation, with the heady, sickly scent of dog breath and hairspray. It seemed to suffocate the whole city.

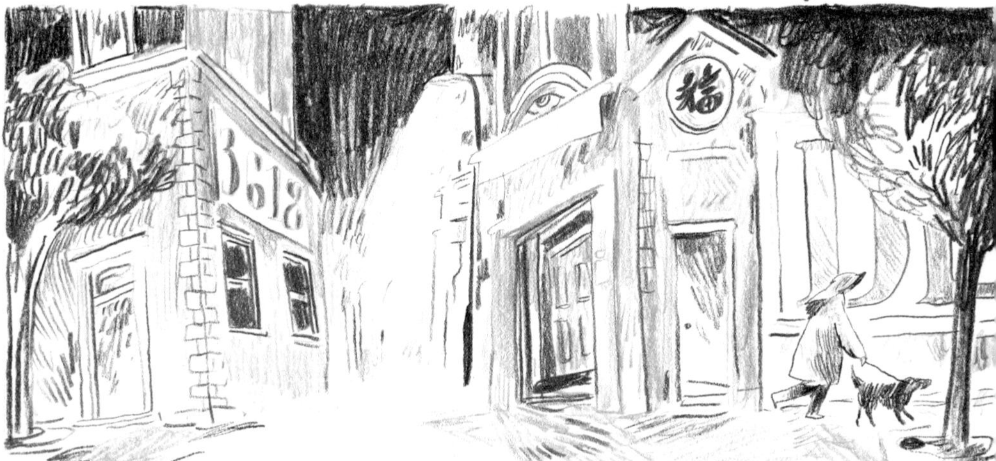

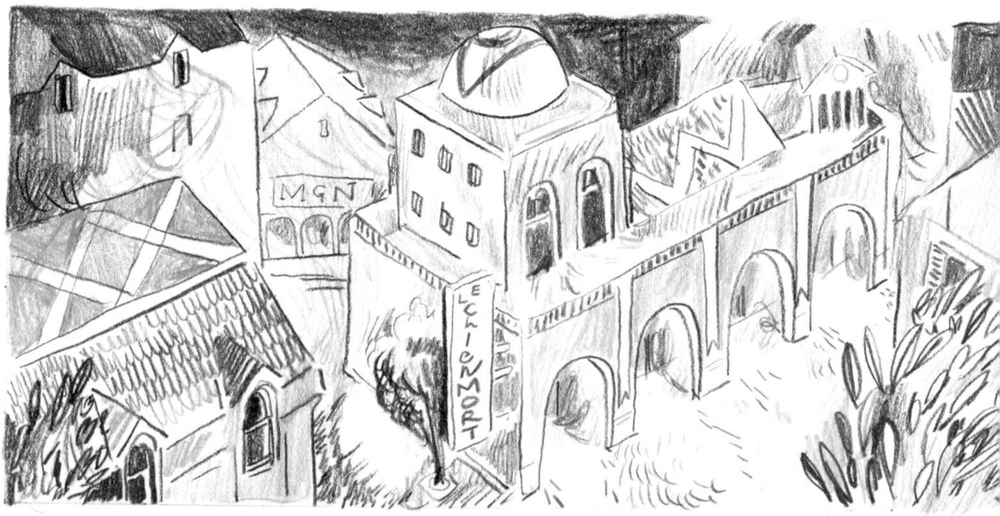
MGN
LE CHIEN MORT

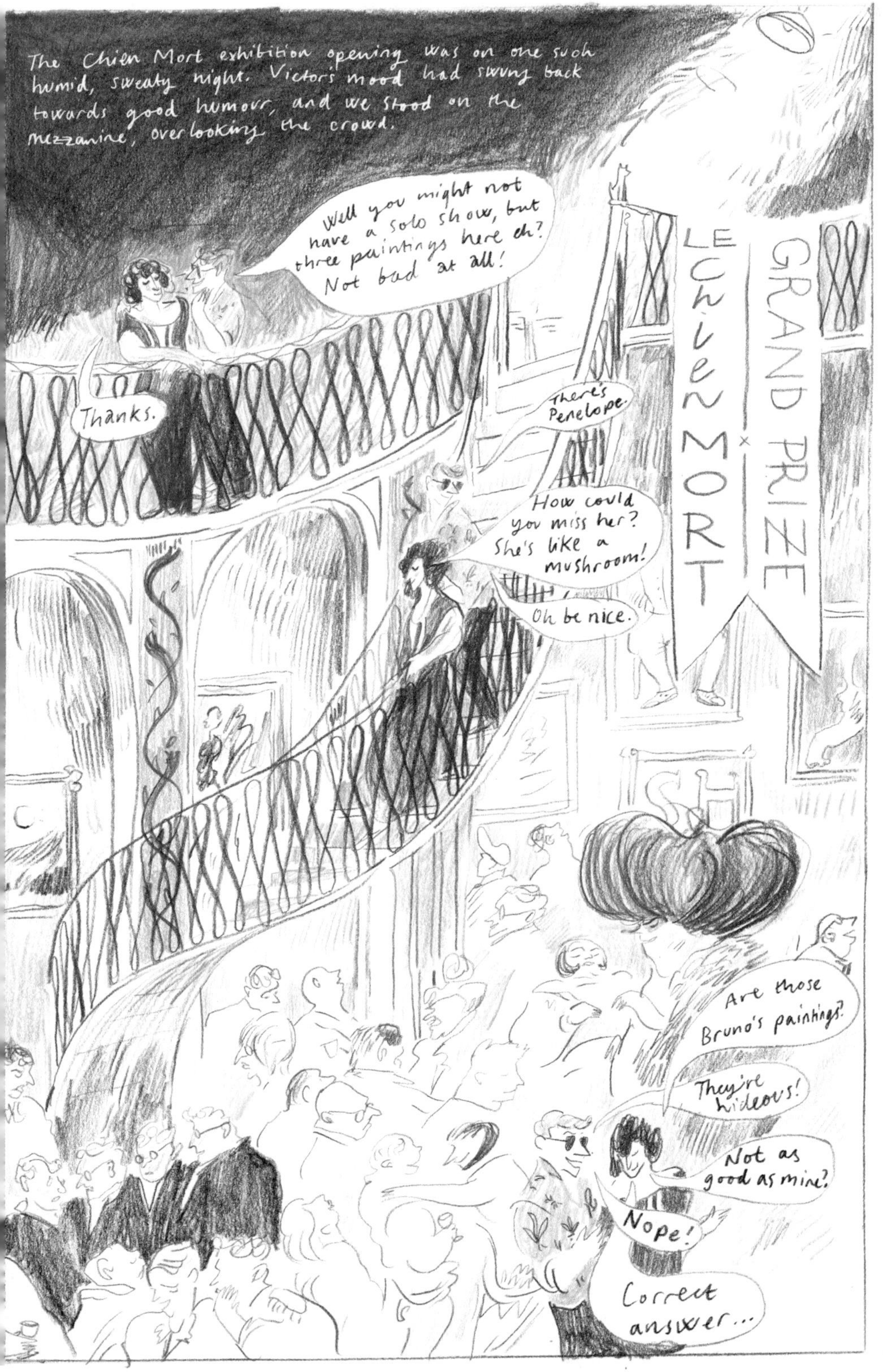

The Chien Mort exhibition opening was on one such humid, sweaty night. Victor's mood had swung back towards good humour, and we stood on the mezzanine, overlooking the crowd.
Well you might not have a solo show, but three paintings here eh? Not bad at all!
Thanks.
LE CHIEN MORT × GRAND PRIZE
There's Penelope.
How could you miss her? She's like a mushroom!
Oh be nice.
Are those Bruno's paintings?
They're hideous!
Not as good as mine?
Nope!
Correct answer...

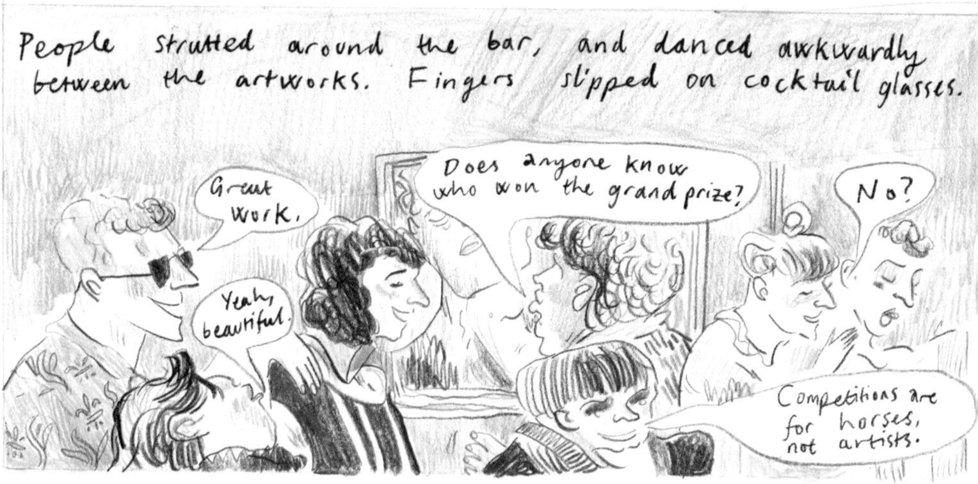
People strutted around the bar, and danced awkwardly between the artworks. Fingers slipped on cocktail glasses.
Great work.
Yeah, beautiful.
Does anyone know who won the grand prize?
No?
Competitions are for horses, not artists.

I saw Stal in the band sweating, his shirt stuck to his chest. Everyone was sweating. The guitars were slightly out of tune.

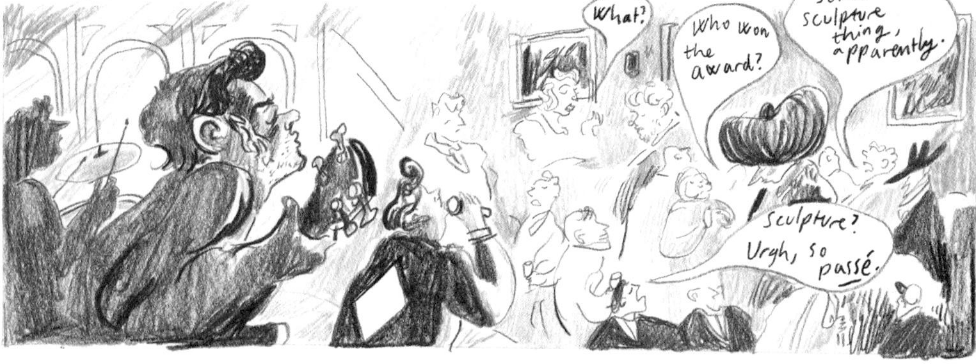
What?
Who won the award?
Some sculpture thing, apparently.
Sculpture? Urgh, so passé.

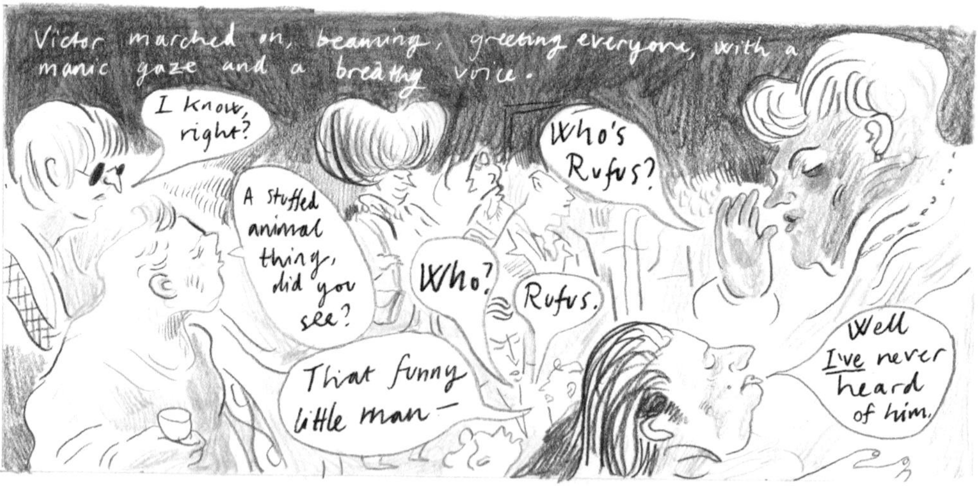
Victor marched on, beaming, greeting everyone, with a manic gaze and a breathy voice.
I know, right?
A stuffed animal thing, did you see?
Who's Rufus?
Who?
Rufus.
That funny little man—
Well I've never heard of him.

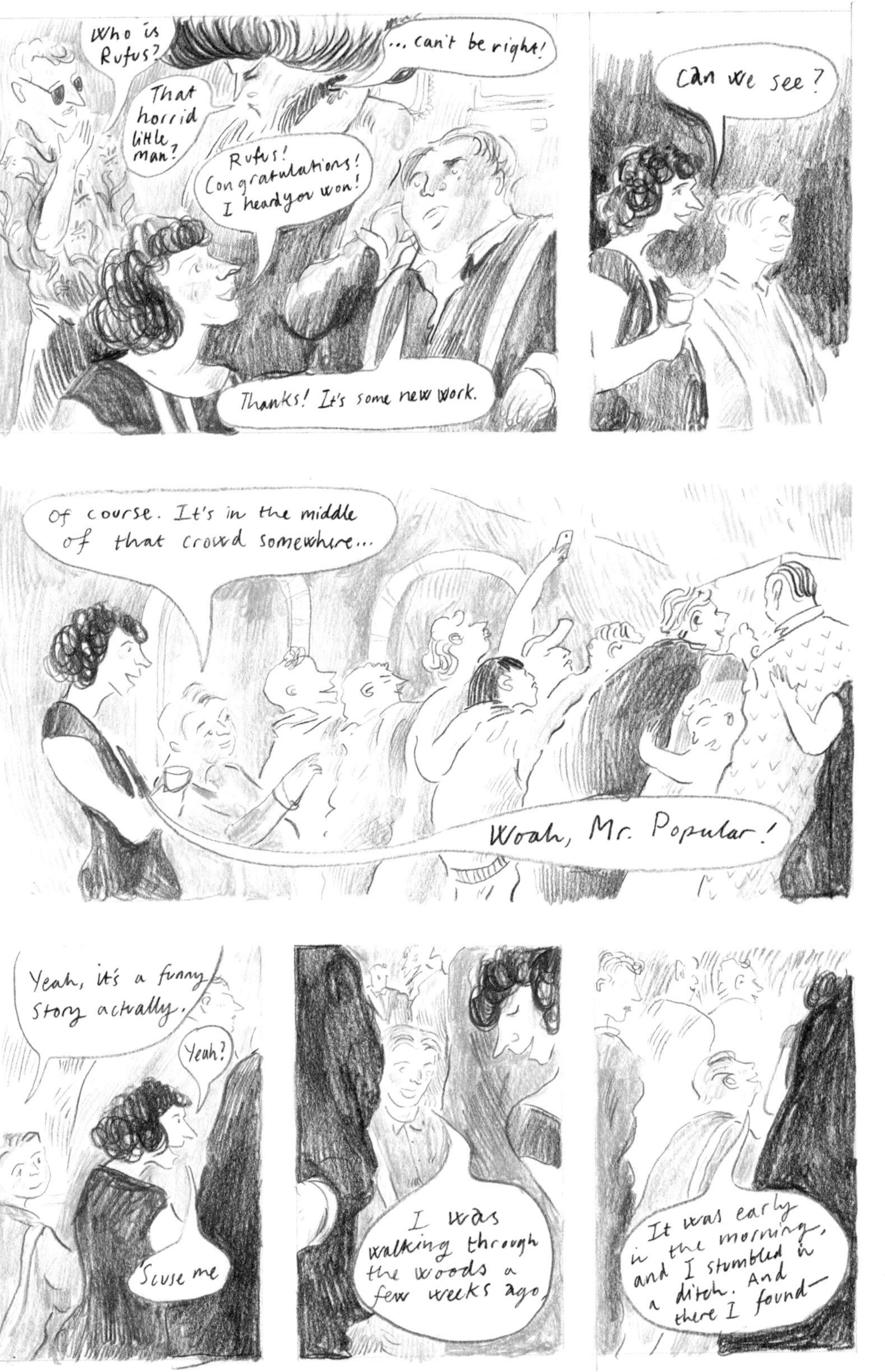
Who is Rufus?
... can't be right!
That horrid little man?
Rufus! Congratulations! I heard you won!
Thanks! It's some new work.
Can we see?
Of course. It's in the middle of that crowd somewhere...
Woah, Mr. Popular!
Yeah, it's a funny story actually.
Yeah?
'Scuse me
I was walking through the woods a few weeks ago,
It was early in the morning, and I stumbled in a ditch. And there I found—

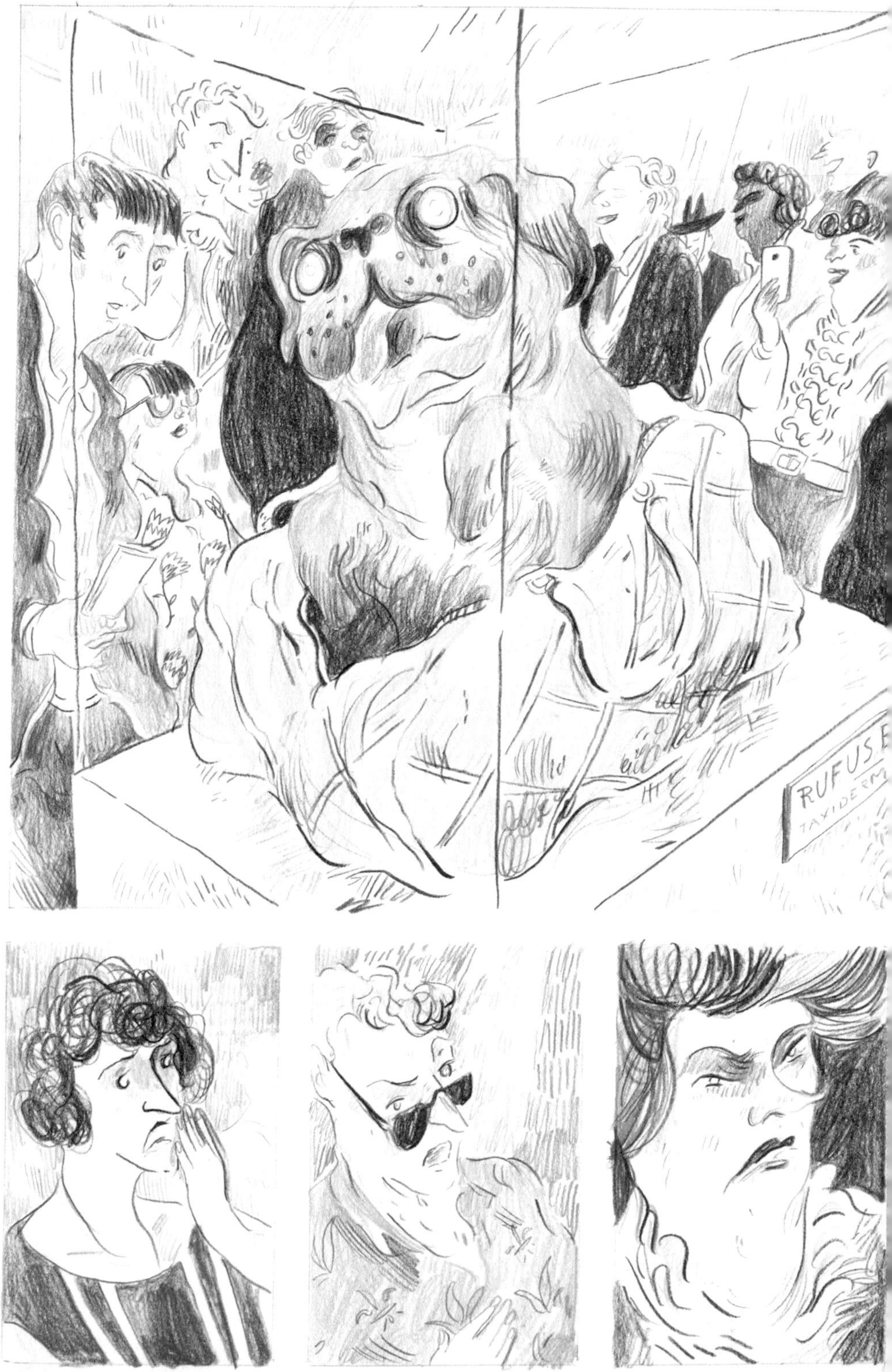
RUFUS E
TAXIDERM

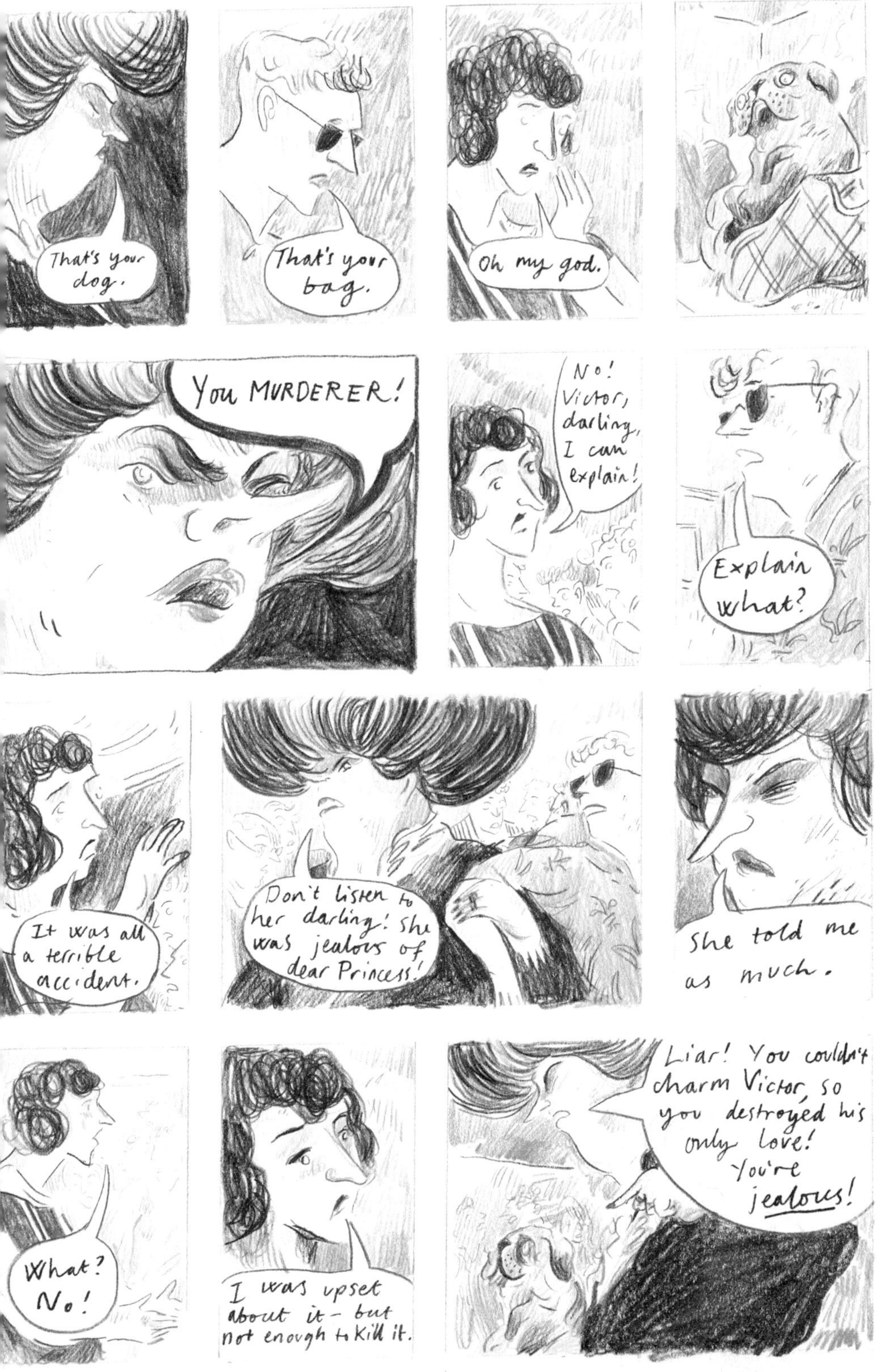
That's your dog.
That's your bag.
Oh my god.
You MURDERER!
No! Victor, darling, I can explain!
Explain what?
It was all a terrible accident.
Don't listen to her darling! She was jealous of dear Princess!
She told me as much.
What? No!
I was upset about it - but not enough to kill it.
Liar! You couldn't charm Victor, so you destroyed his only love! You're jealous!

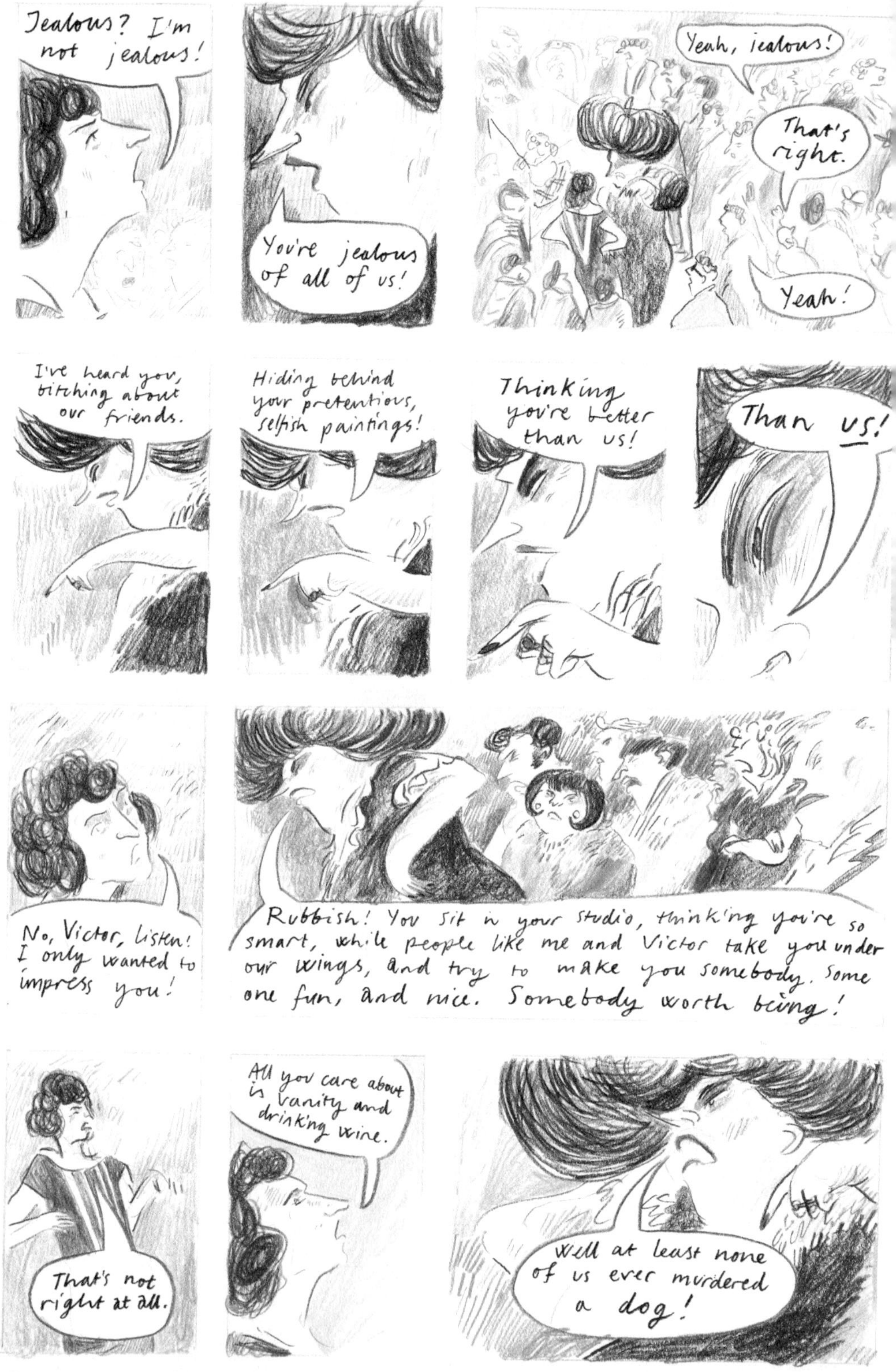
Jealous? I'm not jealous!
You're jealous of all of us!
Yeah, jealous!
That's right.
Yeah!
I've heard you, bitching about our friends.
Hiding behind your pretentious, selfish paintings!
Thinking you're better than us!
Than US!
No, Victor, listen! I only wanted to impress you!
Rubbish! You sit in your studio, thinking you're so smart, while people like me and Victor take you under our wings, and try to make you somebody. Some one fun, and nice. Somebody worth being!
That's not right at all.
All you care about is vanity and drinking wine.
Well at least none of us ever murdered a dog!

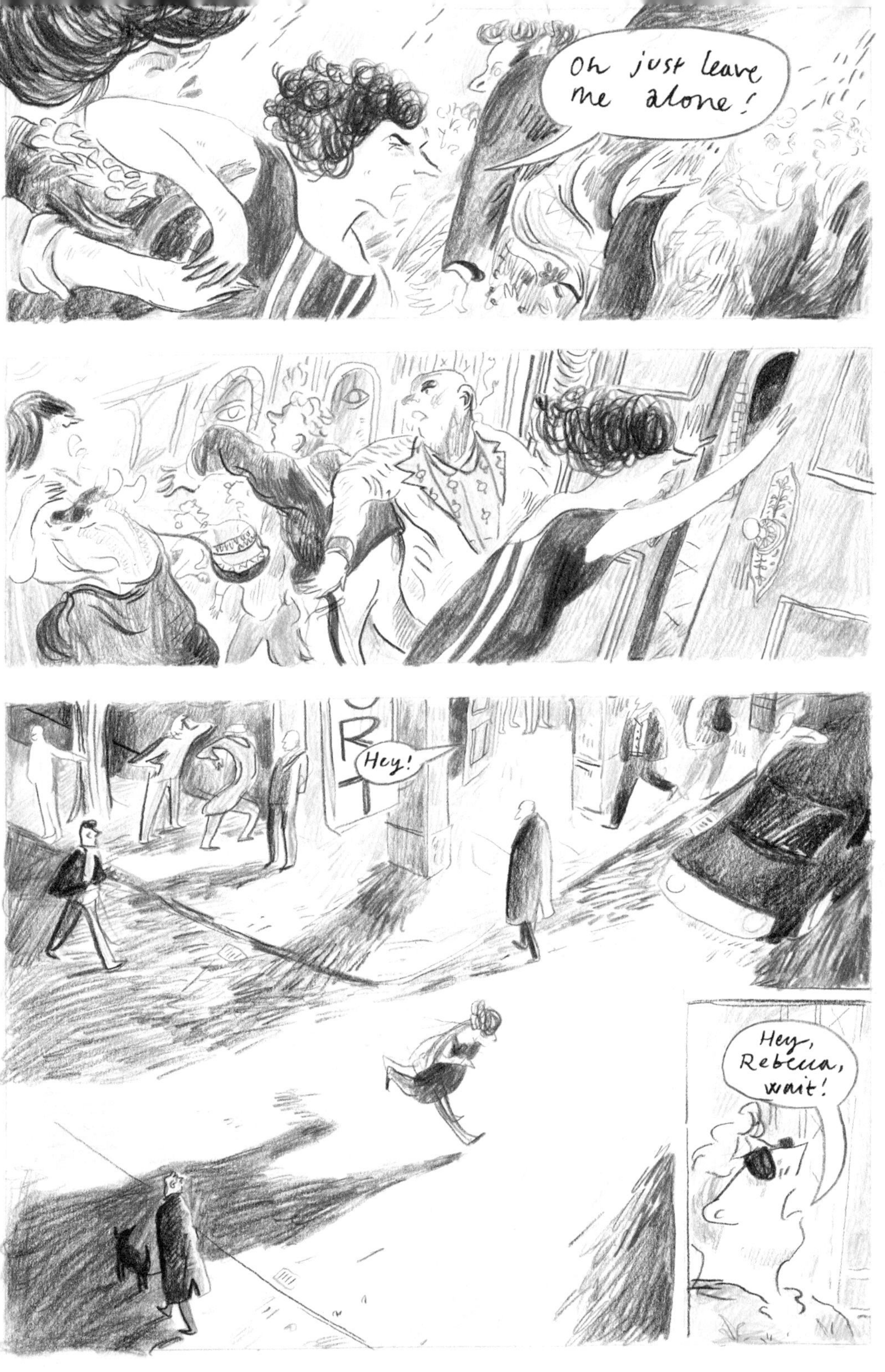
Oh just leave me alone!
Hey!
Hey, Rebecca, wait!

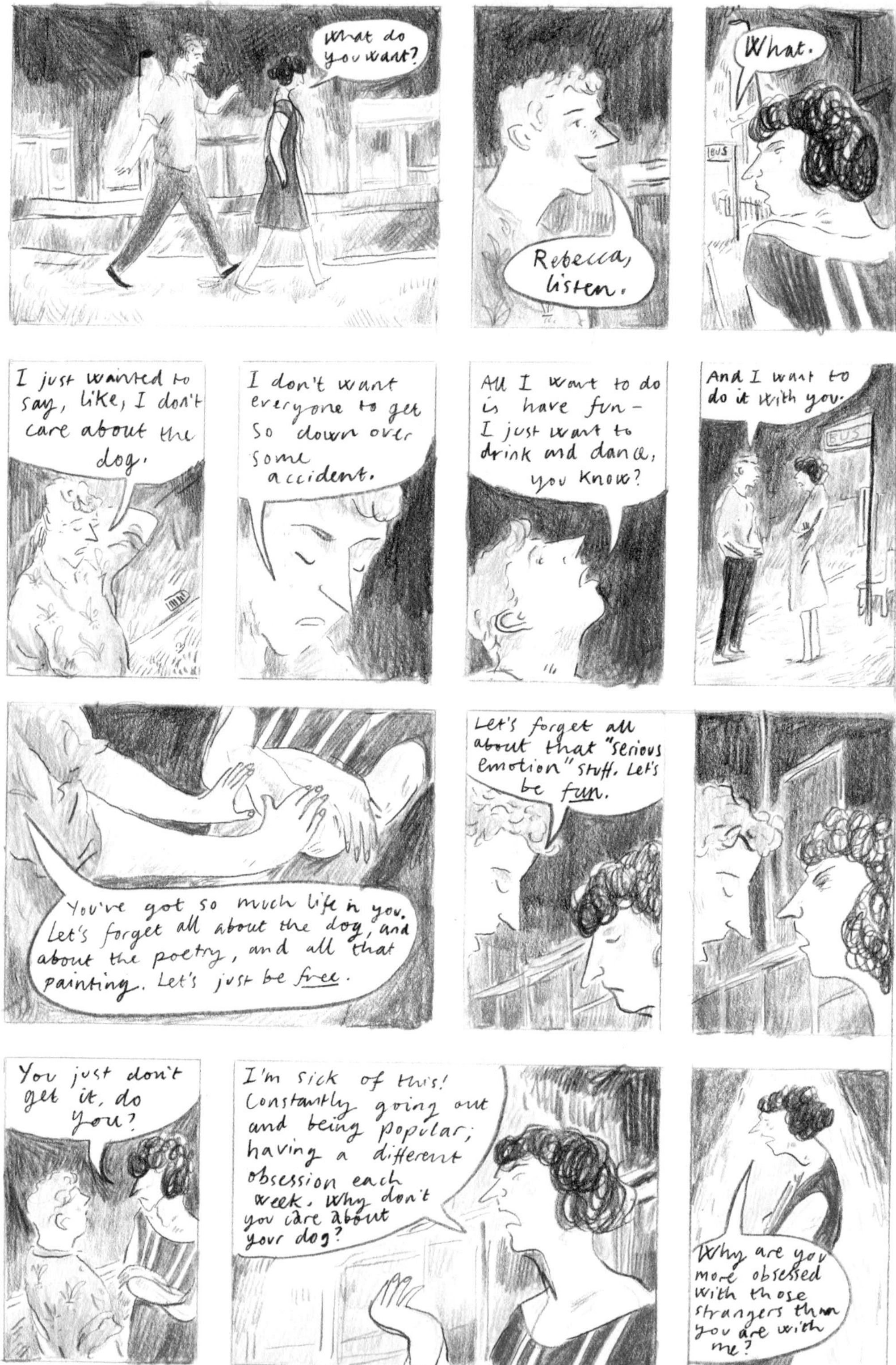
What do you want?
Rebecca, listen.
What.
I just wanted to say, like, I don't care about the dog.
I don't want everyone to get so down over some accident.
All I want to do is have fun – I just want to drink and dance, you know?
And I want to do it with you.
BUS
You've got so much life in you. Let's forget all about the dog, and about the poetry, and all that painting. Let's just be free.
Let's forget all about that "serious emotion" stuff. Let's be fun.
You just don't get it, do you?
I'm sick of this! Constantly going out and being popular; having a different obsession each week. Why don't you care about your dog?
Why are you more obsessed with those strangers than you are with me?

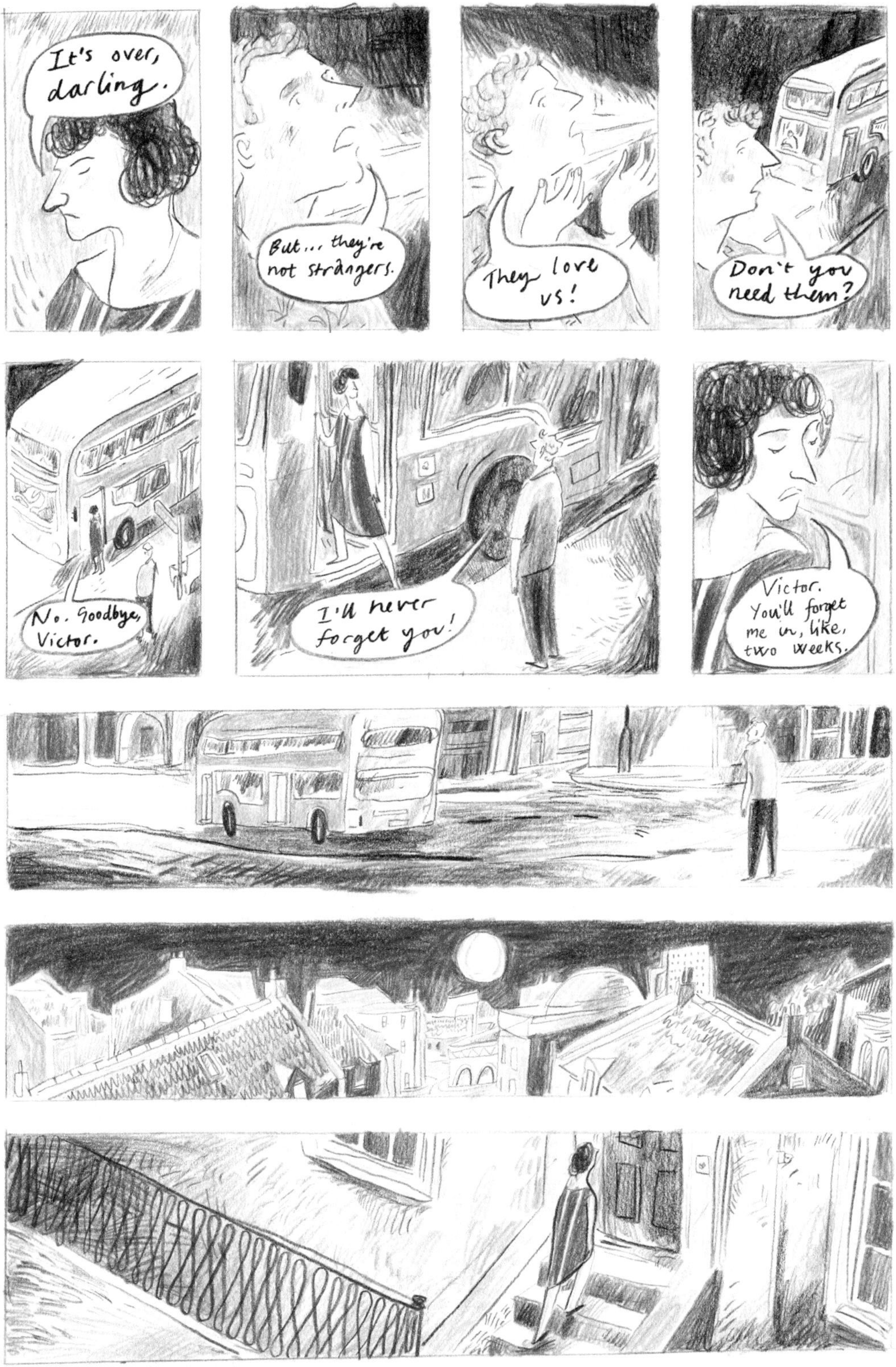
It's over, darling.
But... they're not strangers.
They love us!
Don't you need them?
No. Goodbye, Victor.
I'll never forget you!
Victor. You'll forget me in, like, two weeks.

Back in the flat, I packed my bag, took my portfolio, and drank a generous glass of wine.

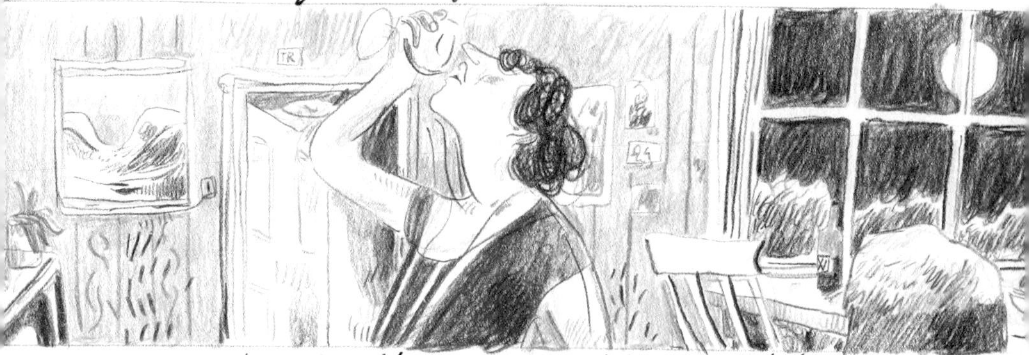

I toyed with the idea of smashing all his possessions, burning his poems, slashing his expensive clothes — of setting fire to the whole place.

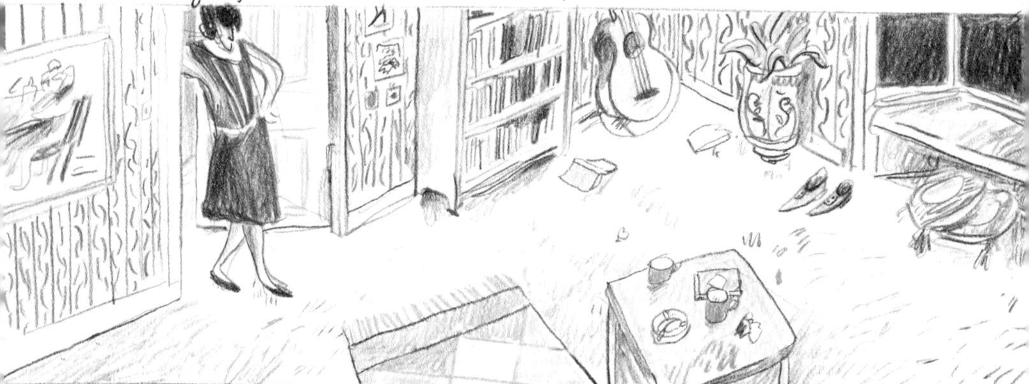

But in the end I pretty much left it. Victor is so fickle, so changeable, so determined to be superficial, that it seems impossible to do any more than the most temporary harm.

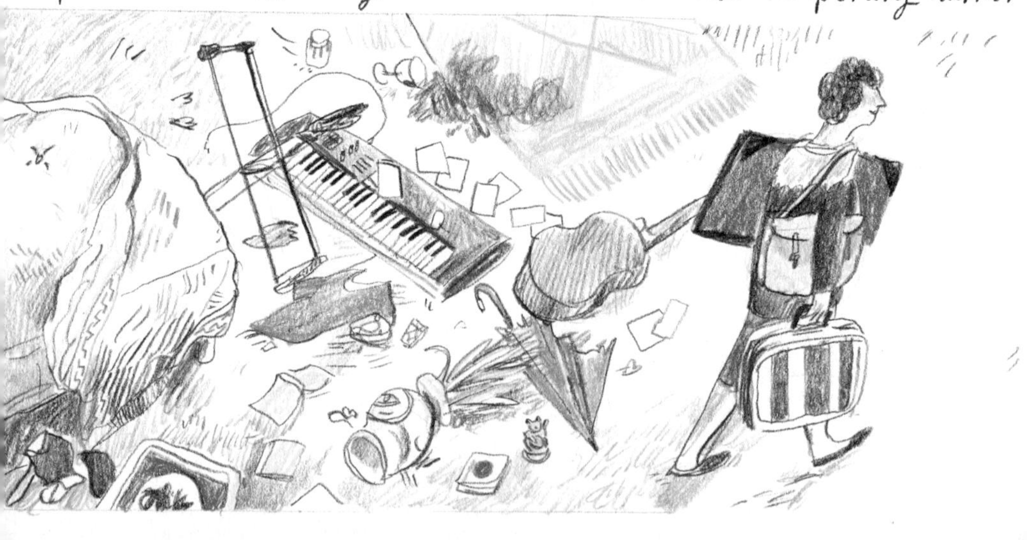

I set off home. Away from the mirage and distractions of Victor and his gang. Away from his changing whims, his attention seeking, and his fleeting passions. Away from the hedonism and the smell of hairspray.

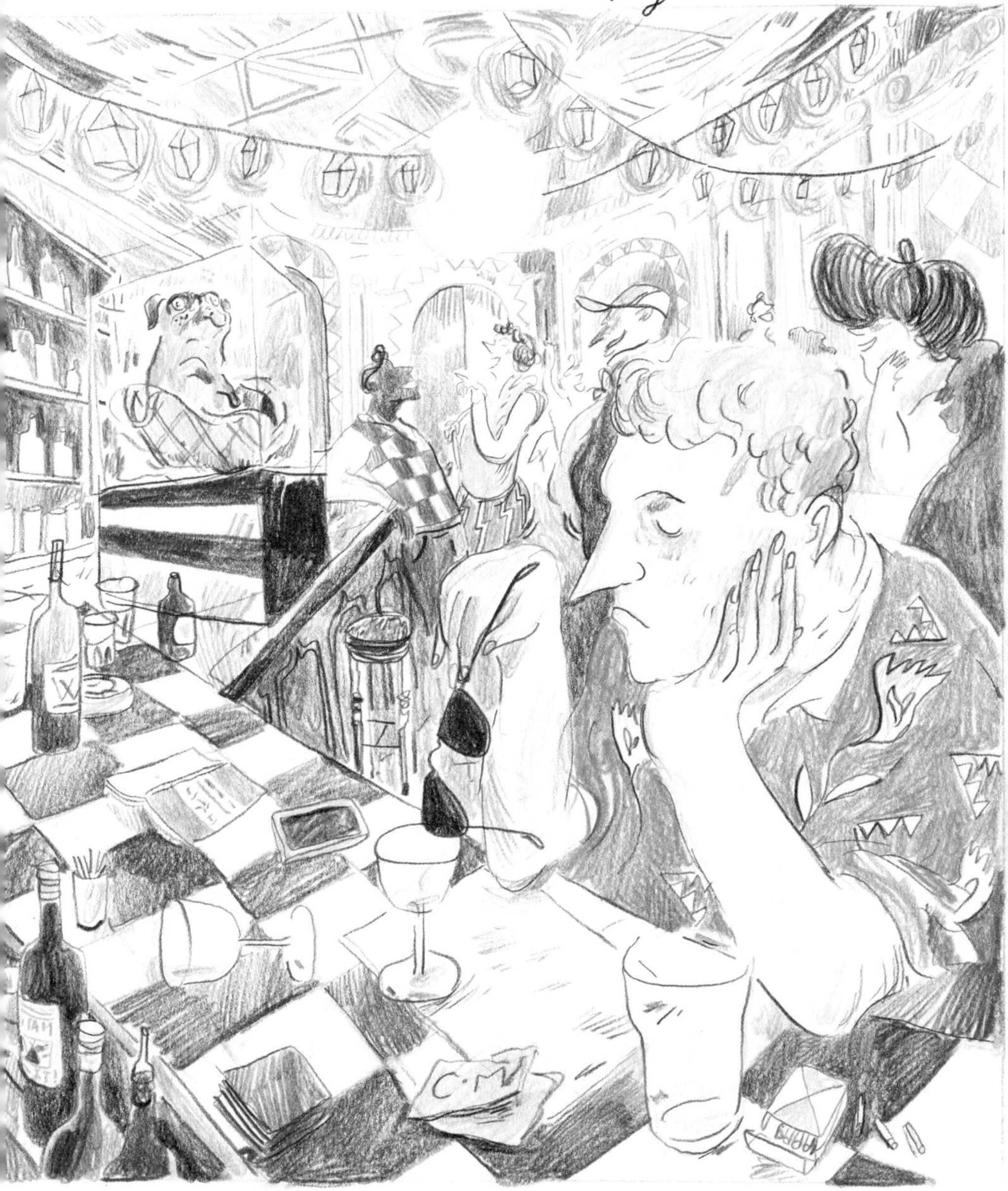
C·M

Later though, I heard from Rufus that the owner of the Chien Mort had bought the taxidermied Princess. It had been installed above Victor's favourite bar. He was forced to see it every single day.

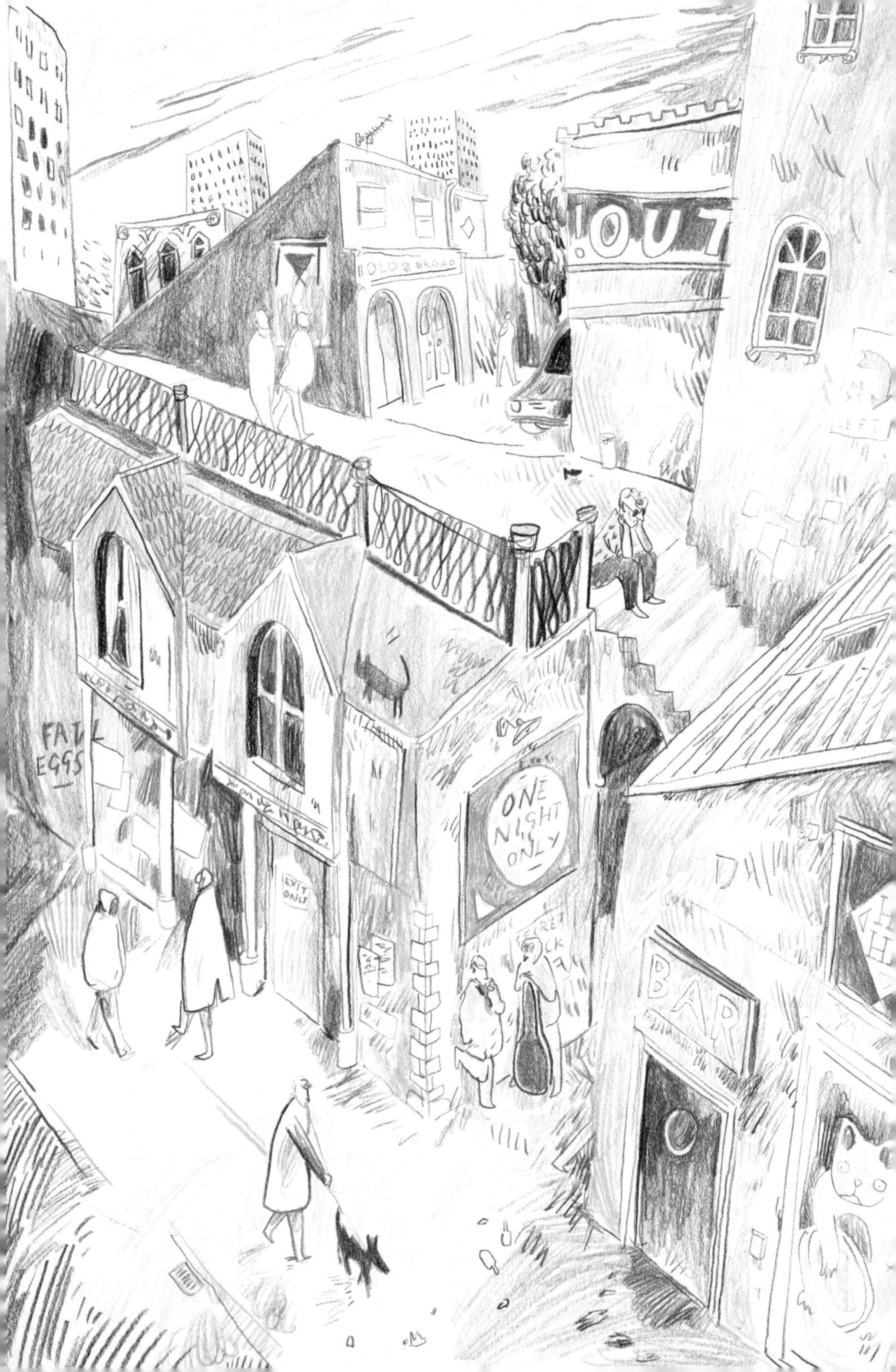
OLD BROAD
OUT
NEXT LEFT
FAT EGGS
EXIT ONLY
ONE NIGHT ONLY
BAR

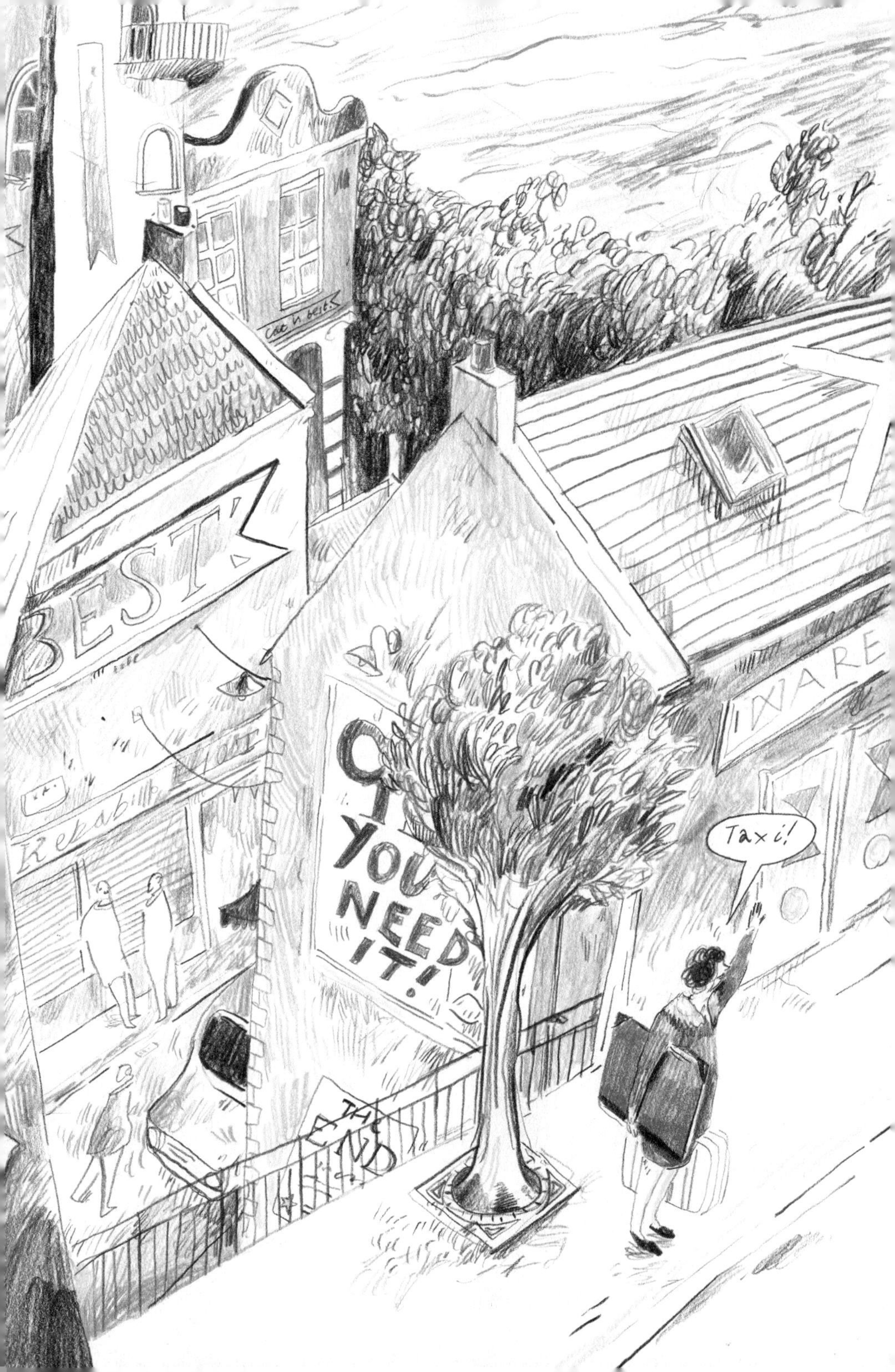
BEST
YOU NEED IT!
THE END
Taxi!

for Cat

Published by Top Shelf Productions, PO Box 1282, Marietta, GA 30061-1282, USA. Top Shelf Productions is an imprint of IDW Publishing, a division of Idea and Design Works, LLC. Offices: 2765 Truxtun Road, San Diego, CA 92106. Top Shelf Productions®, the Top Shelf logo, Idea and Design Works®, and the IDW logo are registered trademarks of Idea and Design Works, LLC. All Rights Reserved. With the exception of small excerpts of artwork used for review purposes, none of the contents of this publication may be reprinted without the permission of IDW Publishing. IDW Publishing does not read or accept unsolicited submissions of ideas, stories, or artwork.

Editor-in-Chief: Chris Staros.

Visit our online catalog at www.topshelfcomix.com.

Printed in Korea.

21   20   19   18   17   5   4   3   2   1